D0955913

THE POWER
OF SIGNIFICANCE

Books by Dr. John C. Maxwell
Can Teach You How to Be a REAL Success

THE POWER
OF SIGNIFICANCE

HOW PURPOSE CHANGES
YOUR LIFE

JOHN C. MAXWELL

**CENTER
STREET**

NEW YORK   NASHVILLE

The author is represented by Yates & Yates, www.yates2.com.

Center Street
Hachette Book Group
1290 Avenue of the Americas, New York, NY 10104
centerstreet.com
twitter.com/centerstreet

Originally published as *Intentional Living* in hardcover and ebook in
October 2015 by Center Street

First edition: May 2017

Center Street is a division of Hachette Book Group, Inc. The Center Street
name and logo are trademarks of Hachette Book Group, Inc.

The publisher is not responsible for websites (or their content)
that are not owned by the publisher.

The Hachette Speakers Bureau provides a wide range of authors for
speaking events. To find out more, go to www.HachetteSpeakersBureau.com
or call (866) 376-6591.

Library of Congress Cataloging-in-Publication Data has been applied for.

ISBNs: 978-1-4555-4821-7 (hardcover), 978-1-4555-4822-4 (ebook),
978-1-4555-7121-5 (large print)

Printed in the United States of America

WOR

10   9   8   7   6   5   4   3   2   1

Contents

Acknowledgments

Thank you to:

Charlie Wetzel, my writer

Stephanie Wetzel, who edits my first drafts

Linda Eggers, my executive assistant

1

Start Writing Your Significance Story

What do you want in life? I believe that no matter what, deep down we all want the same thing. We want our lives to matter. We want our life stories to be of significance. We want to find our purpose—our individual way of making the world a better place—and to live it to the fullest.

You have it within your power to make your life a great story, one guided by your unique purpose and leading to significance. Every person can. Regardless of nationality, opportunity, ethnicity, or capacity, each of us can live a life of significance. We can do things that matter and that can make the world a better place. I hope you believe that. If you don't now, I hope you will by the time you're finished reading this book.

Don't let the word *significance* intimidate you. Don't

let it stop you from pursuing a life that matters. When I talk about significance, I'm not talking about being famous. I'm not talking about getting rich. I'm not talking about being a huge celebrity or winning a Nobel Prize or becoming the president of the United States. There's nothing wrong with any of those things, but you don't have to accomplish any of them to be significant. To be significant, all you have to do is make a difference with others wherever you are, with whatever you have, day by day.

Not long ago I read *A Million Miles in a Thousand Years* by Don Miller. He eloquently writes about seeing our lives as stories. He explains, "I've never walked out of a meaningless movie thinking all movies are meaningless. I only thought the movie I walked out on was meaningless. I wonder, then, if when people say life is meaningless, what they really mean is *their* lives are meaningless. I wonder if they've chosen to believe their whole existence is unremarkable, and are projecting their dreary lives on the rest of us."[1]

If you are reading these words and thinking to yourself, *That's me. My life is meaningless. It has no purpose. My existence is unremarkable,* then I have good news for you. This doesn't have to be your story.

No matter what your beliefs are, I can tell you this. If your story isn't as meaningful or significant or compelling as you want it to be, you can change it. You can begin writing a new story, one with purpose, beginning today.

Don't settle for being merely a teller of stories about significance. Decide to *be* the story of significance. Become the central character in your story of making a difference!

That's what I want for you. I don't want you to be merely a *storyteller* of significance. I want you to be a *story liver*! Your story still has many blank pages. You can write on them with your life.

How to Start Writing Your Significance Story

If you're like me and want to make a difference and have a significance story to tell by the end of your life, I can help you. I'm going to show you a pathway toward identifying and pursuing your purpose. But first, you need to be willing to take an important step forward. And that comes from a change in mindset. You need to embrace responsibility for finding your purpose and being the "writer" of your story. Here's how:

1. Put Yourself in the Story

No one stumbles upon significance. We have to be intentional about making our lives matter. That calls for action—and not excuses. Most people don't know this, but it's easier to go from failure to success than from excuses to success.

Look at the lives of people who have achieved significance, and you can hear them calling you to put yourself into your story. Perhaps they didn't use those exact words, but if you look at what they've said, you can sense the call to action:

> "To dare is to lose one's footing momentarily. Not to dare is to lose oneself."
> —Søren Kierkegaard

> "If you aren't in over your head, how do you know how tall you are?"
> —T. S. Eliot

> "Be the change you want to see in the world."
> —Mahatma Gandhi

People ask me all the time for advice about how to write a book. I tell them to start writing. Many people would love to write a story, a poem, or even a book, but they never do. Why? They're afraid to start. To figure out what you are meant to do, you have to start doing. Stop looking—start living! Dive in! You never know how well you can swim until you are in over your head.

2. Put Your Purpose in Your Story

A well-written story is built using elements that people think are important. When you live your purpose, you are telling people around you that significance is important to you. Almost everyone wants to live a life of meaning and significance, whether or not they express the desire.

To pursue your purpose, you must do things out of your comfort zone. And you must make changes that you may find difficult. We often avoid trying to make those changes. But know this: though not everything that we face can be changed, nothing can be changed until we face it.

To pursue your purpose, you must also take action. Being passive may feel safe. If you do nothing, nothing can go wrong. But while inaction cannot fail, it cannot succeed either. We can wait, and hope, and wish, but if we do, we miss the stories our lives could be.

We cannot allow our fears and questions to keep us from seeking our purpose. Are you tempted to wait until an ideal time? Do you worry that if you start on this journey without knowing exactly where it will go you might not do well? Are you concerned that you might fail?

Let me help you by telling you something you need to know. You won't do well the first time you do anything. You don't know what you're doing when you start. Nobody is good at the beginning of doing something new. Get over it. If you want to live a life that matters, don't start when you get good; start now so you become good.

Everyone starts out bad, regardless of what they're practicing for. We start so we can improve. We start before we're ready because we need and want to get better. The idea is to deliver our best each time we try until one day, we become good. And then one day, we may even have a chance to be great. That's growth. But we can't evolve if we don't start.

Your story won't be perfect. A lot of things will change. But your heart will sing. It will sing the song of significance. It will sing, "I am making a difference!" And that will give you satisfaction down to the soul level. I'll show you how to tap into your purpose in the next chapter.

3. Stop Trying and Start Doing

"I'll try my best." This is a statement most of us have made at one time or another. It's a way of saying, "I'll work at having the right attitude and I'll work at the task, but I won't take responsibility for the outcome." But is *trying* to do your best enough for a life of significance? Can we move from where we are to where we want to be just by *trying*?

I don't think so.

Trying alone does not communicate true commitment. It's halfhearted. It is not a pledge to do what's necessary to achieve a goal. It's another way of saying, "I'll make an effort." That's not many steps away from, "I'll go through the motions." *Trying* rarely achieves anything significant.

If an attitude of *trying* is not enough, then what is?

An attitude of *doing*!

There is enormous magic in the tiny word *do*. When we tell ourselves, "I'll do it," we unleash tremendous power. That act forges in us a chain of personal responsibility that ups our game: a desire to excel plus a sense of duty plus complete aliveness plus total dedication to getting done what has to be done. That equals commitment.

An attitude of *doing* also helps us to become who we were meant to be. It is this *doing* attitude that often leads to the things we were meant to do. While *trying* is filled with good intentions, *doing* is the result of intentional living.

Your story, like mine, won't be perfect. Everyone's stories include wins and losses, good days and bad, highs and lows, surprises and uncertainties. That's life. This book is not about creating a *perfect* life for you. It's about discovering a *better* life for you.

I've been an observer of people all my life, and I've noticed that most people are pretty passive about their lives. An indication of this is that when asked to describe significant regrets in their lives, eight out of ten people focus on actions they did *not* take rather than actions they *did*. In other words, they focus on things they failed *to* do rather than things they failed *at* doing. A better story will emerge for you when you are highly intentional with your life. I know because I have experienced it.

Your Best Story

As you think about your life story and how you want it ultimately to read, I want to leave you with a final thought. I often teach that we have two great tasks in life: to find ourselves and to lose ourselves. Ultimately, I believe we find ourselves by discovering our *why*. We lose ourselves while traveling the path of significance by putting others first. The result? The people we help also find themselves, and the legacy cycle can begin again. That cycle has the power to live on after us. When I die, I cannot take with me what I have, but I can live in others by what I gave. This is what I hope for you as you read this book.

If you're ready to learn how purpose changes everything, then turn the page and let's look at how finding your *why* helps you find your way.

2

Find Your *Why* to Find Your Way

If you want to make a difference and live a life of significance, you find your *why*. You need to tap into your purpose. I'm certain everybody has one. Your *why* is the life's blood of your ability to achieve significance.

If you know your *why* and focus on going there with fierce determination, you can make sense of everything on your journey because you see it through the lens of *why*. Once you find your *why*, you will be able to find your *way*. How do those things differ? *Why* is your purpose. *Way* is your path. When you find your why, your path automatically has purpose. And life becomes much more meaningful and complete because you have context to understand the reason you're on the journey in the first place.

During a Q&A when I was teaching on this, someone

asked, "Does the *why* always have to come first? Can you find your way and then find your *why*?"

You may be wondering the same thing. What has to come first? The good news is that either can come first. But if the *why* comes before the *way*, your ability to tap into the power of significance will come more quickly and immediately be more effective.

Think of it like this. Have you ever wondered why people often find great joy in packing for a vacation? They spend weeks building up great anticipation, looking forward to those warm days on a tropical beach or trips down the slopes of their favorite ski resort. So they pick out each item that goes into the suitcase with great care.

When you get ready for a trip, almost all of your effort is focused on the purpose of the trip. That's why it's a lot more fun to pack for a trip than it is to unpack afterward. This concept applies more broadly to our lives. Whatever path you travel, you're going to be able to do things more significantly because you understand your purpose for being there.

To give you another example, let me share with you how I first began to figure out my *why* after I had started on my *way*. I graduated college in 1969 and started my career as a pastor of a tiny church in Hillham, Indiana. At that point, the model I had in my mind for helping people was the traditional picture of a shepherd. That's how pastors were trained back then. The emphasis was on feeding and caring for the flock, protecting them and keeping them together. That matched my heart for the people of Hillham, whom I immediately fell in love with. But I soon discovered that image didn't fit my gifts and temperament. I was not a natural shepherd. I was more of a *rancher.*

What do I mean by that? I cared *about* people, but I was not content to merely care *for* people. I didn't get excited about sitting around the campfire with existing members and singing "Kumbaya." My real passion was to reach new people and invite them to join us. I wanted to march onward with Christian soldiers and take new territory. I wanted to build something. I wanted to be a pioneer and a leader.

That quickly prompted me to begin asking myself some soul-searching questions that I hadn't expected so soon in my career.

Was I doing something wrong?

Should I change?

Did I miss my calling?

During this time of questioning, I read a book called *Spiritual Leadership* by J. Oswald Sanders. In this book, Sanders writes about the need for vigorous, talented leaders in the church and presents the key principles of leadership in both the earthly and spiritual realms. He illustrates his points with examples from Scripture and the biographies of other eminent men of God, such as David Livingstone and Charles Spurgeon.

The message of the book was another eureka moment for me in my journey of significance because I suddenly realized my gifting called me to become a leader— someone who innovates and takes new ground—rather than a pastor who cares for people. I started to look at myself and my calling differently. My thinking was starting to change, and my horizons were starting to expand. Something was stirring within me. It was making me think more about what I was doing, and more important, *why*.

Then one Sunday morning, someone came into our church in Hillham holding a bulletin with a picture of a church he'd been to in Hammond, Indiana.

"I went to services here last week," the man said excitedly. "They've got four thousand people in their congregation!"

Wow! I could hardly fathom that. In college, when I had been encouraged to set some goals, I dreamed of someday, by the end of my career, having a church of five hundred people. It was as big as I could imagine. Now I was hearing about a church eight times the size of that. It struck a chord deep within me. It challenged and inspired me.

"Can I have that bulletin?" I asked.

He gave me the bulletin, and I taped it to a folder that

I carried around with me every day for the next several years. Whenever I looked at it, I'd say to myself, "I can do this. I am going to build one of the largest churches in America. I will do this." Several times a day, every single day, I fed my mind, body, and spirit with the belief that I had the power and capacity to turn that dream into a reality. I was convinced it was possible. How could I have such confidence? I was beginning to tap into my *why*.

When you start your day with your *why,* you will find yourself continually doing things that inspire you. That is certainly true for me. Finding my *why* gave me the focused and driven energy that I still feel today.

I'm convinced that most people want to live a life of purpose. The vast popularity of Rick Warren's book *The Purpose Driven Life* was in part based on this desire, which became evident when millions of people bought the book. Rick writes, "Humans were made to have meaning. Without purpose, life is meaningless. A meaningless life is a life without hope or significance. This is a profound statement and one that everyone should spend time pondering. God gives purpose. Purpose gives meaning. Meaning gives hope and significance. There is awesome truth contained within that logic."

Just think of the difference knowing this message would make to a young person just starting his or her life. When I read Rick's book, it was an affirmation of how I have lived. I got so excited about it that I wanted to buy it and give it to every twenty-year-old I knew. Purpose empowers significance.

How Your *Why* Helps You Find Your Way

If you tap into your *why*, your life will open up to significance. It will be within your reach every day because you will be able to do simple things that matter. Significance is usually not a result of anything spectacular. It's based on small steps in line with purpose. Knowing your *why* helps you to know what to do and to follow through. Here's how:

1. Knowing Your *Why* Allows You to Focus More on Others and Less on Yourself

Purpose comes from within. It works from the inside out. What happens when you don't know your *why*? You have to spend a lot of time looking within yourself to find it, and trying new things to see what fits you and what doesn't. There's nothing wrong with that. How else will you know what's important to you? But it takes time. It requires effort. You need to ask yourself lots of questions. And all the while, your focus will be on yourself.

The sooner you know your why, the sooner you can shift your focus from yourself to others. The sooner you can just get on with it. You can lose yourself in others. That is where significance lives and thrives.

We all have to find ourselves before we can lose our-selves. If you are preoccupied with trying to understand your personality, identify your talents, and learn the basics in your skill set, it's hard to think about others. Know yourself and settle your *why*, and you'll have the capacity to focus on others.

2. Living Out Your Why Gives You a Confidence That Is Attractive to Others

Knowing my *why* gives me great security and comfort in everything I attempt and do. That confidence and self-assuredness is usually appealing and reassuring to oth-ers, because most people long for it.

Have you ever noticed people who walked into a room and you could feel their presence? They just seemed to know what they were doing and where they were going. They brought energy into the room. It's almost like their presence entered the room before they did. That's not ego or arrogance. It's *purpose*. People with purpose walk with an air of distinction, as if they have a *why* in every step. Wouldn't you like to have that same sense of purpose?

Purpose is the rudder on your boat. It gives you direc-tion and keeps you going in the right direction when the wind is blowing and the waves are crashing against you. It provides calm and confidence in the midst of a storm. People who know their *why* can keep their heads while everything around them is in turmoil. And that draws others to them.

3. The More You Live Your Why, the More You Layer It

People's strengths and their individual purposes are always connected. I embrace that truth because I believe God has gifted everyone with the ability to be great at what they are supposed to do. But you don't have to be a person of faith to make the connection between talent and purpose. Your *why* is fuel for your strengths. And your strengths are the *way* to fulfill your *why*.

Every time you use your strengths to live out your *why*, you build on your strength and increase your *why*. Living this way adds layers of ability, purpose, credibility, and significance to your life. The more you do, the more you learn, because you are layering each experience into your life.

Think about it like this. When you start off doing something, you are usually not very good at it. But with time and practice, you get better. After a while, you create layers of success that you can build on, and you also build up tremendous confidence as a result. That's what great athletes do. They don't start off playing their sport at a professional level. It takes years of practice to get to the highest level. How do they do it? They layer wins, losses, pain, and gain.

Whenever I look up at the majestic Canadian Rocky

Mountains, I am always in awe of their rugged stature and endless beauty. I am aware that every cut I see in the rock is a record of history for that mountain. Each jagged edge tells a story. Thousands, if not millions, of years of sand, soil, and minerals impacted by heat, water, wind, and rain have formed the statuesque vision I see. The horizontal layers show the natural changes that have occurred over time. The layers reflect the formation of that mountain. When you know your *why*, you know the history and purpose of each experience in your life.

4. The More You Layer Your Why, the More Impact It Has on Others

Purpose is like a snowball rolling downhill—it builds over time. It compounds. Doing the right thing for the right reason with the right people—over time—gives you a huge significance return, and ultimately a giant significance reputation. Why do I say that? Because I've experienced it. I've given my life to helping others, and because I've stuck with it, people recognize me for it.

Most people want to see a high return on their efforts right away. They want to be given reputation credit in advance. That's not how life works. You have to earn credibility. Keep acting according to your purpose and doing significant acts day by day, year by year, decade after decade, and your impact will keep increasing. Will you be able to see that increase every day? Maybe not.

But it will be there. And remember: a day of significant living may be delightful, but a lifetime of significant living can be magnificent.

5. Knowing Your *Why* Keeps You in the Game Longer

Have you ever known someone who died soon after retiring? I have. Why does it happen? Because people have a harder time living without a *why* to live for. What incentive do people have to keep living when there is no purpose for their actions, no reason to get out of bed each morning?

I don't ever want to retire. I'm like my dad. I want to keep living and giving until I've got nothing left. To this day, my dad's still in the game, and he is ninety-four years old! Every morning he gets up excited. Why? Because he still has his *why!* Every day he visits old people—it never dawns on him that he *is* an old person. Everyone he meets is someone whom he wants to encourage to keep going, to keep focusing on their reasons to live. He makes fifty pastoral visits a week to various homes.

People who know my dad say to me, "You're blessed to have his genes." I agree. But I'm even more blessed to know my *why.* That will sustain me a long time. I'm going to live fully until I die. And God willing, I've still got a long way to go. But when I finally do pass and I am six feet in the ground, I hope they put on my epitaph,

"Here lies a man who lived with purpose and intentionality," because that's how I want to be remembered.

Do you know your *why*? Finding it is usually a process. You probably won't do it overnight, and you won't get the whole thing at once. It comes bit by bit as you take steps forward. That's why it's so important to start small—and it's why I discussed the idea of starting small but believing big in the last chapter, before introducing the idea of finding your *why*. It's almost a catch-22. To find your *why*, you need to take steps forward while believing. But to take steps forward and believe, you need to find your *why*. So which do you do first? Whichever one you can. Do the thing you're best positioned to do.

Everyone Has a *Why*

I believe every person has a *why* and has the ability to find it. Do you believe that too? If not, are you willing to accept the idea? If you haven't already found yours, I believe you can. Why am I convinced of that?

Every person was created to do his or her part to better mankind. That includes you!

Every person has talents that will help him or her better mankind. That includes you!

Every person is given an opportunity to better mankind. That includes you!

Every person has a purpose for which he or she was created. That includes you!

Every person must look within to discover his or her purpose. That includes you!

Maybe you already have a strong sense of your *why*. If so, you already have a great head start on your significance journey. However, if you're like most people, you would be grateful to have some help figuring out your *why*. I want to help you with that.

The process begins with questions. I love to ask questions. They have unlocked more doors of opportunity for me than anything else I have ever done. So I ask questions in any and every kind of situation. And then I listen to the answers. That's where learning begins to happen.

My mother is the one who taught this to me. It seemed she always had time for me. Always. And whenever she gave her time to me, I knew I had her full attention. We would sit down together and she would listen to me, sometimes for hours. She always listened until I was talked out. No interruptions, with continual visual expressions to let me know that she was hearing every word and understanding the feelings that accompanied each idea. She heard with her ears and connected with her eyes. Her heart constantly gave me unconditional love.

Does it sound like she was a saint? She was. She was my mother!

Mom asked questions only when I was finished talking. They were filled with amazing insight because she always heard me out. Her reflective nature allowed her to think through each question she asked and couch it in a context of love. Her questions helped me sort out my feelings and caused me to reflect. It was at her side that I learned to listen and ask questions. My mother passed away in 2009, and I miss her greatly.

The first question you must ask yourself is this: How can I add value to others? If you can quiet yourself enough to listen for that answer from within yourself, you will begin to understand your *why*. I have to tell you that *this question has been the foundation and driver of every significant act in my life*. Did you get that? Having a life that matters comes from the ability to add value to others. This is where significance starts. Let that idea stir within you while I show you more specifically how to find your *why*.

Three Clues to Your *Why*

Back in 1965, when I was studying for my bachelor's degree at Ohio Christian University, a speaker came to my Psychology 101 class and asked us three questions. To this day, these questions have shaped my life. At the time, I was only an eighteen-year-old freshman, and I was not sure of my answers. But the questions stayed with me, and I have revisited them again and again over the years. I'll share them with you now, because I believe they will help you find and better understand your *why*.

Question 1: What Do You Cry About?

This first question asks you to look inside yourself and think about what breaks your heart. What disturbs you? What inflicts emotional pain? What causes you so much discomfort that you are motivated to take action and do something to bring healing to that situation?

When I heard this question at eighteen, I didn't have a clear answer. Today, I do. My heart breaks when I see people falling short of who they could be. People have so much potential, and many fall short and live broken and unfulfilled lives. It brings tears to my eyes.

Because I have gifts and talents in the areas of communication and leadership, I feel a great sense of responsibility to try to help people in this area, to inspire and lead them to change and grow to their potential. I feel the weight of it on my shoulders every day. What does carrying that weight mean to me?

First, it means I am always conscious of my calling to help others find significance in their lives. When I see people, I see their greatest potential. I see them as potential tens. My overwhelming desire is that they see it too. I want them to shake off the mental and emotional shackles that bind them and run the race of life with excellence and exuberance. And any time I can help someone do that, it raises my spirits and makes me think, *I was born for this!*

The second thing I understand about the weight I am carrying is that I must be a voice that calls people to intentional living. And I use the word *call* purposely because for me, it is a calling. I need to give expression to people's longing to make a difference and let them know that it is within their reach. Perhaps that's why I identify with the words of Elizabeth Rundle Charles, who wrote in the *Chronicles of the Schonberg-Cotta Family*, "To know how to say what other people only think, is what makes men poets and sages; and to dare to say what others only dare to think, makes men martyrs or reformers."

The third thing the weight of this calling means to me is that I believe I am supposed to be a catalyst in bringing people together to do significant works. Leadership is my life; I get an enormous charge from casting vision and then bringing people together to reach a level of significance that is impossible without a team effort. It is at the core of my *why*.

So, what makes you cry? What makes your heart break? What touches you at the depths of your soul? Do you already know the answer? Or is it something you need to start exploring and thinking about?

When trying to figure out what makes you cry, you can look at your personal history. You can think back to your childhood. You can tap into social justice issues that get you angry. You can think about the last thing you got highly emotional about—or the thing that you *always* get emotional about. Any of these things can be clues to what makes you tick. And they will help you identify your *why*.

Question 2: What Do You Sing About?

What always makes you happy? What puts a bounce in your step? What makes you jump for joy or spontaneously break into song? Back when I first heard this question, my answers didn't have a lot of depth: good grades, friends, food, and sports. What do you expect? I was only eighteen.

Today, nothing makes me happier than seeing people become intentional about making a difference. I believe this is the key to transforming our world. Poet Ralph Waldo Emerson said, "The purpose of life is not to be happy. It is to be useful, to be honorable, to be compassionate, to have it make some difference that you have lived and lived well." I believe that when people experience what Emerson wrote about, they will discover their greatest joy.

Doing acts of significance brings more deep satisfaction than any other work I've ever known. It fires me up and keeps me going. Even when my schedule is out of control, deadlines are piling up, and the pace of life seems hectic, I seldom feel overworked. As the saying goes, work is not work unless you would rather be doing something else. There is nothing I would rather do than help people make a difference for others.

What do you sing about? What gives you great joy? What feeds your passion? What feeds your soul? What gets you excited?

When I ask, "What do you sing about?" many people respond by thinking about what entertains them. There's certainly nothing wrong with being entertained or having fun. I love to have fun as much as the next person. But what I'm really talking about is something that resonates at a deep level. Something that makes contented joy spontaneously rise up within you. It's the kind of thing you would do for free, just because. Once again, these are clues that help you to understand your purpose and know your *why*.

Question 3: What Do You Dream About?

This last question really expands the possibilities of your life. It capitalizes on the answers to the two previous questions and takes them to the next level by bringing in the "what if" factor. What if you could do anything you wanted to make the world better? What if you could make a difference on a larger scale? What if you could do something significant, something that would impact others and outlast you? This is what keeps me going.

In 1965 as a freshman in college, I knew I wanted to make a difference by helping people, and I wanted to do it as the pastor of a church. But to be honest, back then, I didn't dream big enough. It wasn't long before the results I was getting started to outpace my goals, and I had to reset my thinking. That may also be true for you. That's why I say that we need to start small but dream *big*.

Today, I'm dreaming bigger. I want to help a million people to achieve significance by becoming intentional in the way they live and by transforming the lives of people. And I want others to know about their stories of transformation. My greatest hope is that you will be one of those people. I want you to have a great life, full of meaning and positive impact on others. I want you to achieve a high level of significance.

I believe God gives each person a blank canvas at the beginning of his or her life. He whispers the word "purpose" as He hands us a brush and paint, and He releases us to be the artist of our own lives. He wants you to make a positive difference in the lives of many. No one else can paint your picture. The brush is in your hands; be prayerful and intentional as you choose the colors and make your strokes. As you do, He will watch with great pleasure as you paint your picture of significance.

What could your picture be? What do you dream about? If you could accomplish anything in the world that would make a difference in the lives of others, what would it be? If you could do anything you wanted and knew you wouldn't fail, what would you do? If you could live out your wildest dream, what would that look like?

Some people dream big. In fact, they're long on dreams and short on action. Others never dream. Maybe they think of themselves as pragmatic. Or maybe their hopes and dreams have been smashed by negative experiences, so they're afraid to dream. I hope that doesn't describe you. I hope you're willing and able to dream, and dream big. Even if you decide you don't want to follow through on a particular dream, the process of allowing yourself to imagine great things is good for you. It helps you to understand who you are and why you're here.

Rabbi Harold Kushner writes, "Our souls are not hungry for fame, comfort, wealth, or power. Those rewards create almost as many problems as they solve. Our souls are hungry for meaning, for the sense that we have figured out how to live so that our lives matter, so that the world will be at least a little bit different for our having passed through it." What meaning does your soul crave? How do you want to make a difference in this world? How can you uniquely add value to others? What skills do you have that can help others' lives transform? How can you be significant?

You may not know your whole *why* all at once. I didn't. But as soon as I understood the direction I was meant to go, I was on my way. After that, it was just a matter of refining my *why*, which continues to happen, even at age seventy. And I hope it will continue to grow, evolve, and sharpen. That is my signal that God's not done with me, and there are still things for me to do and ways for me to make a difference in this world.

Significant Application:
Find Your *Why* to Find Your Way

Follow the Clues

To find your *why*, you need to follow the clues that can only be found inside of you. To unlock them, take time to answer the three questions in this chapter:

What do you cry about?
What do you sing about?
What do you dream about?

I strongly encourage you to set aside a block of time to write out your answers to these questions. And I just want to caution you: Don't try to figure out your answers before you write them down. Use the writing process to *discover* your answers. Start by writing whatever comes to mind, and just go with it. There is no right or wrong to this exercise. It's supposed to be a messy learning process. (If you're a person of faith, I also recommend you pray as you do this exercise. Ask God to reveal the clues to you.)

Start with One Word

Another way to help you discover your *why* is to focus on the core of who you are and see what grows from that. In his book *Aspire* Kevin Hall writes, "The first thing I do when I'm coaching someone who aspires to stretch, grow and go higher in life is to have that person select the one word that best describes him or her. Once a person does that, it's as if he or she has turned to a page in a book and highlighted one word. Instead of seeing three hundred different words on the page, the person's attention, and intention, is focused immediately on that single word, that single gift. What the individual focuses on expands."[2]

What is your one word? What best describes you? That single word may inspire you, focus your attention, and help you to understand your *why*. Where will that one word take you? How does it relate to adding value to others? Why is it significant? Keep that one word in your mind as you go about your day in the coming weeks and see where it leads you.

3

Embrace Intentional Living

Poet Samuel Johnson is credited with saying, "Hell is paved with good intentions." Why would he say such a thing? Isn't it a positive thing to want to do good, to possess a desire to help others? My answer is yes. Having a heart to help people and add value to them makes you a better person. But if you don't act on it in an intentional way, it won't make a difference.

Crossing the Significance Gap

There are many ways to be significant—as many as there are people on earth. Each of us has unique skills, talents, opportunities, causes, and callings. I'll help you start to figure out what some of those things are. Since you're still reading this book, I believe you have made the decision to get into your story as I suggested in chapter one. You want to live a life that matters. You desire significance. That's good. But the next question is how.

First, let me clarify what I mean when I talk about *intentional living.* I'm describing a life that brings you *daily satisfaction* and *continual rewards* for merely working to make a difference—small or large—in the lives of others. Intentional living bridges the gap between your purpose and a life that matters. Good intentions won't get you there.

What's the big difference between good intentions and intentional living? I can show you using just a few words. Take a look at the three columns of words below, and as you do, ask yourself, "Do I live in the land of good intentions, or in the land of intentional living?"

Words of Good Intention	Words of Intentional Living	A Life that Matters
Desire	Action	Results
Wish	Purpose	Fulfillment
Someday	Today	Every Day
Fantasy	Strategy	Follow-Through
Hopefully	Definitely	Continually
Passive	Active	Proactive
Occasional	Continual	Habitual

Emotion	Discipline	Lifestyle
Somebody Should	I Will	I Do
Survival	Success	Significance

As you look at these lists, can you see why good intentions alone will never get you to significance? In fact, if all you ever do is cultivate good intentions, but you never act with intentionality, you're actually likely to become more frustrated and less fulfilled, because your desire for positive change may increase, but the lack of results will leave you frustrated.

Whether we realize it or not, people live in one land or the other. Whether by design or default, if we have a desire to make the world a better place, we either settle for good intentions or embrace intentional living. Which will you do?

Learning to Be Intentional

How did I recognize that intentional living was the key to a life that matters, that it was the bridge between purpose and significance? When I was in my midtwenties, I met a man named Curt Kampmeier.

Curt was associated with the Success Motivation Institute out of Waco, Texas. Because I had heard him talk about the principles of success and I really liked what he had to say, I had written him a note asking to meet with him the next time he came through my town. Much to my surprise, he said yes. So we met for breakfast.

While I was eating my eggs, Curt asked me if I had a personal plan for growth for my life. It was a question nobody had ever asked me. Not only didn't I have one, I didn't even know I was supposed to have one. I was so embarrassed by the question that I tried to fake my response. I started to tell him about all the things I was doing in my work and how many hours I put in. He saw right through it.

"If you're going to grow," he said, "you have to be intentional."

That statement hit me like a punch in the face.

Curt told me he had a detailed plan for growth—a kit with material on goals and attitude and initiative and responsibility. I knew instinctively that these things could help me. When I asked him how I could get it, he told me I could purchase it for $695.

That was the equivalent of one month's salary for me!

I went home from breakfast looking for alternatives. I started asking friends and colleagues if they had a plan for growth. Nope. None of my friends was intentional about becoming better at what he did. They just expected it to happen on its own, like I had. That sounds kind of like good intentions, doesn't it?

Finally, my wife, Margaret, and I sat down, put pencil to paper, and figured out how to sacrifice and pinch our pennies to save the money to buy the kit. We were newly married then, barely scraping by on the money we were making. Yet at the end of six months, we'd saved what we needed. (Realize that this was in the days before credit cards were available to everyone.)

I'll never forget the day I received the kit. I had seen it before when I met with Curt, but when I opened it and started to dig into it, I was struck by the simplicity of it. At first I thought, *I paid almost $700 for this?* I had been hoping for a silver bullet. Instead, this was going to require a lot of work.

What else could I do? I dove in. After all, we'd spent a small fortune for the kit. But it wasn't long before I realized it was worth every penny. Yes, it encouraged me to dream, but it also taught me to put details to my dreams and attach deadlines to them. It prompted me to examine myself and where I was. It called me to look at my strengths and weaknesses. It made me identify my goals every week. And it engaged me in a process of growth every day.

I had hoped for a solution. Instead, it gave me direction.

It was a course in intentional living. Even buying the kit had forced me to be intentional, because we had made sacrifices every day for six months to save the money for it.

That kit helped me begin creating my first life plan. I cannot put a price on how valuable it was. Why? Because it led to a major epiphany:

If I wanted to make a difference...

Wishing for things to change wouldn't make them change.
Hoping for improvements wouldn't bring them.
Dreaming wouldn't provide all the answers I needed.
Vision wouldn't be enough to bring transformation to me or others.
Only by managing my thinking and shifting my thoughts from desire to deeds would I be able to bring about positive change. I needed to go from wanting to doing.

Maybe you've already had this epiphany yourself. Maybe you've already begun to make this shift. Maybe you figured it out earlier than I did. But if you didn't, guess what? You can make the change from good intentions to intentional living right now. In fact, you can become so intentional in the way you live that your friends and loved ones, your colleagues and bosses, your neighbors and naysayers will say, "What in the world happened?" Your transformation will blow their minds. And it will inspire others to embrace intentional living, too.

The Seven Benefits of Intentional Living

Intuitively, you might sense that intentional living would benefit you, but I'm guessing you'd also like to know specifically what it does for us. My experience has shown me that it does many things for us. Here are seven of its benefits:

1. Intentional Living Prompts Us to Ask, "What Is Significant in My Life?"

Living intentionally will motivate you to start asking questions and begin prioritizing whatever is important to you. That's what it did for me. I began by asking how I could be successful. When I had begun to achieve some success, I realized that I needed to be asking questions about significance.

> *Can I make a difference?*
> *Whom should I help?*
> *How can I help them?*
> *How can I add value to them?*

These questions began to help me become intentional in my purpose and in the area of significance.

Once I asked myself, "What is significant in my life?" and realized the answer was adding value to people, I began to focus on that thought. That's the essence of intentionality. An unintentional life accepts everything and does nothing. An intentional life embraces only the things that will add to the mission of significance.

2. Intentional Living Motivates Us to Take Immediate Action in Areas of Significance

When you have shifted from good intentions to intentional living, whenever you detect a need that matters to you, you no longer think, *Something must be done about that.* Instead, you think, *I must do something about that.* You take ownership. Napoleon Hill said it best when he observed, "You must get involved to have an impact. No one is impressed with the won-lost record of a referee."

We all have a tendency to put off things. But no people have ever thought themselves into significance. They acted themselves into it. You can't sit in the bleachers— you've got to get in the game. Allow the desire to act that you feel when you become intentional to propel you into acts of significance. The most important thing you can do is to get started because it will increase your appetite for more significance.

3. Intentional Living Challenges Us to Find Creative Ways to Achieve Significance

When you live an intentional lifestyle, you see many possibilities. When you are unintentional, you see few:

Intentional living always has an idea.
Unintentional living always has an excuse.

Intentional living fixes the situation.
Unintentional living fixes the blame.

Intentional living makes it happen.
Unintentional living wonders what happened.

Intentional living says, "Here's something I can do."
Unintentional living says, "Why doesn't someone
   else do something?"

Intentional and unintentional living are worlds apart
in every aspect of life, including creativity.

Intentional living is all about knowing what you
want. Often that desire will be elusive or even seem-
ingly impossible to achieve. However, when we feel that
way, necessity disguised as creativity can kick in. When
it does, intentional living turns the doubt-filled question "Can I?" into the invigorating, possibility-inducing
"*How* can I?" When you know what you want and can't
find what you need, you must create what you need, so
you can get what you want!

4. Intentional Living Energizes Us to Give Our Best Effort to Do Significant Acts

Being unintentional is failing to take aim in life. Unintentional people wander through life without focus.

They are like Brother Juniper in the comic strip by Father Justin "Fred" McCarthy, who shoots arrows at a wooden fence in the backyard. He pulls back the bowstring and lets the arrow fly. Wherever it sticks into the fence, he takes a marker and draws a target around it. This way, he figures he is sure never to miss a bull's-eye.

Sadly, many people live their lives similarly, landing somewhere random and calling it a bull's-eye. That describes life without purpose or energy. Living that way would be like golfing without the hole, playing football without the goal line, playing baseball without home plate, or bowling without the pins.

For anything to have great meaning, it needs to be driven by a specific objective and followed through with action. We know this when we're trying to win the one we love before we get married. When we're dating, the pursuit of the other person is usually highly intentional. We try to maximize every experience with the person. We do extra things and go out of our way to please him or her. We look our best. We're on our best behavior. We try to make our loved one's day. Sadly, after the marriage, many people lose that intentionality and focus on the other person, and they spend their time waiting for the other person to make their day. That's when the relationship begins to slide.

Of course, intentionality can take us in the wrong direction when our focus is off. I learned that on my wedding day. After the ceremony, Margaret and I were packing the car to leave for our honeymoon. We planned to drive to Florida to stay at her grandparents' house for a week. As I was loading our luggage, Margaret saw me placing not one but *two* briefcases in the trunk.

"What are those, John?" she asked.

"I thought I'd bring along some work to do in my spare time," I said, pleased with myself for being so strategic.

I didn't think it was possible, but with both irritation and flirtation, she said. "Honey, there'll be no spare time!" I'd tell you she was right, but that's none of your business! Let's just say that as we packed the car, she was already trying to teach me an important lesson in intentional living.

5. Intentional Living Unleashes the Power of Significance within Us

It is a law of nature that you cannot reap without sowing. That's why it's so important to give first, before you expect to receive. The compounding, positive result of practicing this principle for many years has now given me an immeasurable return on my investment into people's lives. People are not only making a difference, but they are also investing in others who are making a difference. I'm seeing season after season of harvest in the lives of others.

This give and take is natural, like breathing. You take in air; you blow it out. You can never just breathe in. Nor can you just breathe out. Both are continually essential. Likewise, we give to others and receive from them. Our lives are to be like a river, not a reservoir. What we have should flow through us to others. The moment the good things we have to offer begin flowing from ourselves to others, the miracle of intentional significance begins to happen. The more we share, the more we have. The more we have, the more we can give. We don't hand out significance in little doses over time. We unleash it. That's how we build a life that matters.

6. Intentional Living Inspires Us to Make Every Day Count

John Wooden, who mentored me for several years, admonished everyone to make every day their masterpiece. This legendary coach of the UCLA Bruins once explained, "As a leader of my team, it was my responsibility to get the most out of my players. As a coach, I would ask myself every day, 'How can I make my team better?' I concluded that my team would improve when each player improved, and that only would happen when each player each day intentionally made that day his masterpiece."

How did Coach do that? Every day during practice he would watch the energy, focus, and overall behavior of each player. If a player was not giving his best, he would walk over to him and say, "I can tell you are not giving a hundred percent of yourself to practice today. I know you are tired, perhaps you stayed up late studying, or maybe this day has been a difficult one. I also know you are thinking *I'm only giving 60 percent today, but tomorrow I will give 140 percent and make up for today.* I want you to know that thinking will not make you a better player. You cannot give 140 percent tomorrow. The best any of us can give on any day is 100 percent. Therefore, if you give only 60 percent today you will lose 40 percent and never recover it. A few days of less than 100 percent and you will be just an average player."

Coach's teaching motivated me to write the book *Today Matters.* The thesis of that book states, "The secret of your success is determined by your daily agenda." The key is to make good decisions based on your principles and values, and then to manage those decisions every day. When I wrote that book, I considered the lessons to be simple and basic. But the teachings of John Wooden were simple, too. He focused on fundamentals, yet he was immensely successful. The key is in the consistent follow-through.

7. Intentional Living Encourages Us to Finish Well

Someday I'm going to die. You are too. What do you want people to say about you at your funeral? I hope people tell funny stories about me. But I also hope they tell a story of significance. I don't want my family and friends to have to guess about my legacy. I want them to tell about how I added value to leaders who multiply value to others. That's the legacy I'm living to create. I believe that's the best contribution I can make while I'm here.

We've all heard the saying, "All's well that ends well," but I believe nothing can end well unless it *starts* well. If you want a life that matters, you don't need to change everything in your life. The shift I am inviting you to make is not huge—but to live a life that matters, it is essential. It is the shift from good intentions to intentional living. That small tweak in your mindset will bring massive significant dividends.

Are you ready to take that step? It's simpler than you might imagine. You just need to align your thinking and your actions. That's what I did. When I recognized I had a choice to be intentional, good intentions no longer ruled my life. You have the power to choose which category to live in, and I want to show you how to get there, how to be intentional and achieve significance.

What will this look like for you? Your journey will probably be similar to mine in some ways. It will be filled with wonderful surprises, great excitement, big changes, unanticipated growth, fond memories, and, hopefully, a tremendous level of inner fulfillment.

However, it will also be vastly different from mine. It will be as unique as you are. Your life's purpose will be deeply personal and special. So will your expression of significance. I believe becoming highly intentional will be the beginning of a whole new world of opportunity for you.

Most people fear that significance is out of their reach. It's not. Anyone can be significant. But it requires embracing intentional living. Are you willing to make the shift from good intentions to intentional living?

If you are willing to make this shift, then let the following pages be your guide to the life you've always wanted but never thought was possible. Once you enter that pathway, your life will really begin to matter to you and to others. Please hear me: Significance is within your grasp. All you need to do is be willing to take the steps.

Significant Application:
Embrace Intentional Living

When we make a judgment call about ourselves, we tend to give ourselves the benefit of the doubt. We know what our *intentions* were, so even if we fall short in our execution, we cut ourselves some slack. That's both good and bad. The good is that it allows us to remain positive and bounce back from failure. The bad is that we aren't holding ourselves accountable for following through, and a life of significance is impossible for anyone who doesn't live intentionally day after day.

Where Do You Fit on the List?

Earlier in this chapter, I introduced you to lists of words that illustrated the differences between good intentions and intentional living. Take another look at them. Put a check next to the word in the left or middle column on each line that better describes your attitude and actions.

Words of Good Intention	Words of Intentional Living	A Life that Matters
Desire	Action	Results
Wish	Purpose	Fulfillment
Someday	Today	Every Day
Fantasy	Strategy	Follow-Through

Hopefully	Definitely	Continually
Passive	Active	Proactive
Occasional	Continual	Habitual
Emotion	Discipline	Lifestyle
Somebody Should	I Will	I Do
Survival	Success	Significance

Unless you checked every entry in the middle column, you still have work to do when it comes to shifting your mindset from good intentions to intentional living.

For every entry where you checked the left column, write a sentence or two describing what you must do to embrace the attitude and demonstrate the actions of intentional living so that you get the results in the right column.

4

Be Willing to Start Small

My discovery of the power of significance didn't truly begin until I decided I wanted to make a difference in the lives of others. I vividly remember the day that I became conscious of that desire. I was in the fourth grade and was walking across a campground with my father.

At that time Dad was an overseer of two hundred pastors in a very small denomination. Although he was in a leadership position over people, the position he had in their hearts superseded any formal position or authority he held. Dad was a constant encourager. He truly loved people and wanted to help them. On this particular day it took us thirty minutes to walk a hundred yards because people kept stopping Dad along the way. They were thanking Dad for kind things he had done for them and passing along thoughtful words.

I listened to the people speak so well of him, and even in those moments his focus was still on encouraging each and every person. I watched their faces as my dad talked to them, making his way across the grass, and I could see that he was lifting them higher than they could lift themselves. When I saw what that did for other people, I knew that I wanted to provide that same gift to people as well. I can remember thinking, *I want to be like my dad. I want to help people, too.*

This is where my desire to make a difference was birthed. As I reflect on that moment of realization, it provides clear evidence that you don't have to be a big person to have a big idea. After all, I wasn't anyone out of the ordinary. I was just a kid from southern Ohio. But something caught fire in my belly that day, and I inherently trusted that I had the capability to touch people's hearts in the same way my dad did. I hoped that if I believed in myself enough, others might be willing to believe in me too. The only way I knew to do that was to follow in my dad's footsteps and enter the ministry. I wanted to lead with conviction, show kindness to others, and offer compassion wherever I went. I would study to become a pastor and be guided by the Golden Rule: Do unto others as you would have them do unto you.

While I considered myself to be an ordinary boy, I recognize that my childhood was filled with extraordinary opportunities most children rarely receive. Because of my father's work, he had developed friendships with many noteworthy spiritual leaders from all over the world. So I was exposed to their teachings at a very young age. While I couldn't possibly appreciate the impact they would have on my life in those moments, I can surely look back now and recognize the effect they had on my path. Each one of these encounters left a lasting impression that shaped my life and my future toward intentionality and significance.

One of those important encounters happened when I was around twelve years old. My father took me to hear Norman Vincent Peale speak at the Veterans Memorial Auditorium in Columbus, Ohio. Dad was a big Peale fan. He was drawn to his messages about the power of a positive attitude. Dad had all of Peale's books in his library, and I had been encouraged to read them time and time again.

After hearing Peale speak, I immediately understood the attraction. I still remember walking down the wide concrete steps of Veterans Memorial Auditorium after that experience. My father turned to me and said, "Norman Vincent Peale is a great man, John, because he helps a lot of people."

By my teenage years, I was ready to tell my father about my desire and intentions to follow in his footsteps, to enter the ministry. The day I told my father how I felt, that I intended to enter the ministry, he put his arm around me and said, "That's wonderful, son." I could see that it touched his heart. He simply yet poignantly looked at me and asked, "What does that mean to you?"

"I am going to give my life to helping people."

He watched me closely, as if he was waiting to see if I would blink. Perhaps he was looking for signs that I might not be certain of my calling. But I had never been more committed to anything in my life. I didn't break our eye contact because I felt confident. This was what I was meant to do.

Dad smiled and said, "Then you are going to make a great difference, son."

I believe my father took tremendous pride in the idea that I would choose to honor him in such a way. And while it's true that he was my chief inspiration, the thought of helping others and having a positive impact on their lives was the engine that drove my passion the most.

Are You Willing to Start Small?

I believe we all have a longing to be significant, to make a contribution, to be a part of something noble and purposeful. And to make that contribution, we need to be willing to focus on others. We need to give of ourselves. The action of intentionality I talked about in the previous chapter must be guided by the desire to improve the lives of others, to help them do what they perhaps cannot do by themselves. Are you with me?

Many people look at all that's wrong in the world and mistakenly believe that they cannot make a difference. The challenges loom large, and they feel small. And they think they must do big things to have a life that matters. Or they think they have to reach a certain place in life from which to do something significant.

Does that seed of doubt exist in you? Have you ever found yourself thinking or saying, "I will be able to make a difference only when...

I come up with a really big idea,
I get to a certain age,
I make enough money,
I reach a specific milestone in my career,
I'm famous, or
I retire"?

None of these things is necessary before you can start to achieve significance. You may not realize it, but those hesitations are really nothing more than excuses. The only thing you need to achieve significance is to be intentional about starting—no matter where you are, who you are, or what you have. Do you believe that? You can't make an impact sitting still.

Every big thing that's ever been done started with a first step. When Neil Armstrong took his first walk on the moon, he stated, "That's one small step for man, one giant leap for mankind." But the first steps of that achievement occurred decades before. We can't get anywhere in life without taking that first small step. Sometimes the step is hard; other times it's easy. But no matter what, you have to do it if you want to achieve big things.

What can you do now? As you think about making a difference, be willing to start small. You never know where your passion-fueled idea might lead. Here are some things that can help you and encourage you to start small but believe big:

1. Start Where You Are

Parker Palmer, a philosopher and author, wrote, "Our real freedom comes from being aware that we do not have to save the world, we must merely make a difference in the place where we live."

Perhaps right now you don't have much, and what little you do possess, you're holding on to for dear life. Let go. You don't need a lot to give. It's a matter of heart and attitude, not how much you have. Are you willing to give that a try? Mother Teresa said that some of the greatest works ever done have been performed from sick beds and in prison cells. Like her, you can be significant from wherever you are with whatever you have.

Opportunity is always where you are. Be willing to start by giving of yourself.

2. Start with Your One Thing

I believe everybody has one thing they do better than anything else. The right place to start is with your one thing. I learned this from my dad. In fact it was a Maxwell house rule when I was growing up. When we were kids, my dad's message to my brother, sister, and me was to find your strength—your one thing—and stay with it. He never encouraged us to try to do lots of different things. He wanted each of us to do one thing exceptionally well. A long running joke in our family was that we felt sorry for multi-gifted people. How would they know which of their gifts to focus on?

In my eyes, my father became an exceptional man not because he was exceptionally gifted, but because he found his one thing and stuck with it. He was a great encourager. As a result, he rose to way above average. He mastered the art of encouraging others and never departed from it. Excellence comes from consistency in using our strengths, and Dad has been consistent.

When I got started doing my one thing, I had no idea it would lead me to where I am today. Besides, even if I'd wanted to start big, I wasn't sophisticated enough to, so I just started with what I had and did it as well as I could. As a result, my ability multiplied. That came from working at it with consistency. I am where I am today, not because I have done several big things, but because I have worked at communicating ever since my twenties, and this intentionality has compounded in my life.

Investing in yourself is like taking a penny and doubling its value every day. If you did that for a month, how much would you end up with? A hundred dollars? A thousand dollars? A million dollars? Not even close.

If you start with just a single penny and double it every day for thirty-one days, you end up with $21,474,836.48. Personal growth is like that. Practice your one thing with excellence daily, and you will get a return. It's like putting money in the significance bank.

What's your one thing? What do you have the potential to do better than anything else? Do you have a sense of what that is? If not, then ask people who know you well. Or look at your history. Or take a personality or skills assessment to get clues. Don't think about what you can't do. Think about what you can. There is always a starting line. You just need to find it. It's about beginning with what you have, not with what you don't have. Find your one thing and start developing it.

3. Start Watching Your Words

Solomon, who was reputed to be the wisest man who ever lived, said, "Words kill, words give life; they're either poison or fruit—you choose."[3] If you want to experience the power of significance and live a life of purpose, you need to embrace some words and reject others. We all have a running dialogue in our heads. What we say to ourselves either encourages us or discourages us. The words we need to embrace are positive, words such as *we*, *can*, *will*, and *yes*. What do we need to eliminate? *Me*, *can't*, *won't*, and *no*.

What kinds of words do you use—in your mind as you talk to yourself, out loud as you speak with others, and in your writing? Are they positive and encouraging? Do they encourage you to embrace a bigger vision? Or are they holding you back? Are they preventing you from doing small things that can ultimately make a big difference? Don't tell yourself that what you can do doesn't matter. It does.

4. Start by Making Small Changes

When Mother Teresa wanted to start her work in Calcutta, she was asked what she must do to consider the work successful. "I do not know what success will be," she replied, "but if the Missionaries of Charity have brought joy to one unhappy home—made one innocent child from the street keep pure for Jesus—one dying person die in peace with God—don't you think…it would be worthwhile offering everything for just that one?"

It's easy to forget that even someone who eventually did big things started out trying to make small changes.

Change can be difficult, but it becomes easier when you do it a little at a time. Nathaniel Branden, who is widely considered to be the father of the self-esteem movement, created what he called the 5 percent practice. He recommended trying to change 5 percent a day by asking yourself a question. For example, "If I were 5 percent more responsible today, what would I be able to do?"

This kind of thinking helps us to embrace incremental change. Trying to make a huge change overnight often creates fear, uncertainty, and resistance, because the change appears unachievable. The idea of making small changes is less threatening and helps us overcome our hesitation and procrastination.

Give it a try. What can you improve by some small percentage? Can you find a way to organize your desk to be more efficient? Can you slightly rearrange your calendar to get more out of your day? Can you become just a bit better at the most important task you do for work? Can you read a book to broaden your thinking ever so slightly? Any small change that makes you better is worth making, because many small changes add up to major improvement over time.

Don't Let Starting Small Stop You from Believing Big

One of the most important steps you can take in life is to increase your belief. If you don't believe you can make a difference, guess what? You won't—no matter how talented you are, how many opportunities you receive, or how many resources you have at your fingertips. You have to believe.

1. Believe in Yourself

Do you believe in yourself? Your belief will drive your behavior. The thought *I don't think I can* often arises out of *I don't think I am.* You will never be more than how you see yourself. Steve Jobs said, "The people who are crazy enough to think they can change the world are usually the ones who do." I've seen many successful people whom others didn't believe in. But I've never met a successful person who didn't believe in him- or herself. Start believing in yourself and you will see a change in your ability to make a difference.

2. Believe in Your Mission

How do you discover your mission? By taking small steps. Too many times people make the mistake of thinking they can discover new experiences, ideas, or concepts without moving. They can't. I've made my greatest discoveries in motion, especially traveling the world. I do my best thinking on the move—not sitting. You're supposed to leave footprints in the sands of time. Most people leave butt prints. You need to get moving. You need to experience new things. You cannot analyze what you don't know. However, the moment you discover something new, your thinking goes to a deeper level.

Let me pause by saying, I am not sure everyone has a mission. I am not even certain everyone has a dream. I used to think everyone did, but now I am not so sure. What I do know is, even people who don't have a dream can connect with someone who does. You can embrace a mission and make it your own.

I believe that's what makes a great cause great. People identify with its goal and want to be a part of it. Just because you aren't leading a mission doesn't mean you don't have a purpose. If you don't feel you have a compelling mission, you can buy into somebody else's cause, make it your own, and still make a difference. You've got to find something that stirs you, even if it's not a mission that started within yourself. It can be a mission that comes from outside you, as long as it's something that you buy into completely and participate in with passion.

3. Believe in Other People

When you work with people who truly believe in you, don't you respond to them based on their level of belief in you? Don't you perform better for a boss you want to please, or for a teacher who encourages you, or for a coach who inspires you? You work harder because of that belief factor.

As you get started in your small efforts to make a

difference, work with people you believe in, people you care about. Or better yet, begin to care about and believe in the people who are already in your life. It will give you the desire to do things for them, to make a difference in their lives.

She Started with a Small Idea

Not long ago I met a young woman named Carrie Rich. In December of 2013, she told me an incredible story.

Though only in her twenties, she was working as a senior director for Inova Health System in Virginia, and one day she got an idea. She wanted to do something positive for others, and she thought that with a small amount of money, she could get others to contribute to organizations that were already making a difference.

She was excited about the idea, so she told her boss, Knox, who had been the CEO of Inova for thirty years. His response was, "That's nice, Carrie, but could you go back to work now?" But then two months later for her birthday, he gave her a card. In it were two things— $100 and a quote attributed to John Wesley: "Do all the good you can. By all the means you can. In all the ways you can. In all the places you can. At all the times you can. To all the people you can. As long as ever you can."

Carrie says that Knox had taken some "lunch money"— the money he would have spent on her birthday lunch—and given it to her to put to good use. So what would she do?

She decided that she would try to turn the $100 into $1,000 for each of six organizations. In today's world where Bill and Melinda Gates have given away $28 billion, that amount probably sounds small. But that didn't discourage Carrie. She wrote to organizations in Washington, DC; Haiti; Tanzania; and elsewhere to ask what they would do with $1,000. The DC-area organization said it could improve literacy rates for a class of students. The Haitian organization said it could sustain ten families by using community agriculture. The Tanzanian organization could send twenty-five women through secondary school.

These stories ignited Carrie's passion. She was ready to act. But how? How could she turn $100 into $6,000? She decided to do something she had never done before. She wrote individual e-mail requests to family and friends—ultimately to every name that came up from her contacts list as she typed alphabetically in the "To" field. She even decided to write to the names that popped up that she didn't recognize. As she came to the "Subject" field, she wondered what to write. When she could come up with nothing better, she wrote, "The Global Good Fund."

It wasn't long before money started coming in: $20, $50, $1,000. "It was extraordinarily generous," says Carrie, "particularly from my peers who were just starting in the workplace. It really resonated with them."

Within two weeks, Carrie had received $6,052. She felt good. She had started small, but she had accomplished her goal. She was ready to give the money to the six organizations. *All done!* she thought. Little could she guess what would happen next.

As the donations were coming in, she had also received an e-mail from someone she had met for five minutes at a conference a year earlier. They had exchanged cards that day, and Carrie had sent him a "nice to meet you" e-mail afterward. That was why his name had been in her contacts. The return e-mail from the man, who wanted to remain anonymous, said, "I'd like to donate a million dollars to the Global Good Fund. Where should I send the check?"

Carrie's reaction: "This guy's pranking me. I'm not giving him my home address!"

She e-mailed him back saying that if he was serious, he was to meet her on a particular day at a specific time in a specific place (a very public one with security cameras). And she would wait only ten minutes.

When he arrived, he handed her a bank-certified check for $1 million, made out to "The Global Good Fund," an organization that did not exist. And his question for Carrie was the same one she had asked the six organizations: What will you do with this money?

Carrie had not prepared for such a question because, honestly, she didn't think the guy would show up. She couldn't fathom someone she'd met for five minutes doing that. She quickly thought about what had made a difference in her life, and she told him she would invest in young leaders around the world who were using entrepreneurship for social impact. As others had invested in her, she would help these leaders to grow personally so that they could be a gift to society. He handed her the check.

Not knowing what to do, Carrie went back to her office and asked to see her boss, Knox. His assistant, Carol, could see that Carrie was sweating and hyperventilating, so she escorted her right in.

"Look what you've done," she said, slamming the check down on his desk. "You gave me the lunch money, and this stranger gave me a million dollars for an organization that doesn't even exist! I have no idea what to do with the money. Would you please help me?"

"I'll help you under two conditions," said Knox. "First, while you may report to me at work, I'd like to report to you at the Global Good Fund. Second, I'm going to match the initial gift."

Carrie says, "You know that expression, 'You fell out of your chair?' I literally fell. Carol came in and she helped me back up. And that's how it started."

That was in 2011. A year later, she stopped working for Inova and became the CEO of the Global Good Fund, which she created as a nonprofit organization. She has begun a fellowship program and is already investing in nineteen young leaders in countries around the world. And she continues to seek opportunities to make a difference.

How big will the Global Good Fund become? How great an impact will it make? I don't know. Carrie is still young. But does it matter? Carrie has found her *why*. She is making a difference now. She has embraced the power of significance. She is helping people and making the world a better place for her having been in it. And isn't that what matters?

Significant Application:
Be Willing to Start Small

Most people want to believe big and start big, or believe small and start small. It goes against the grain to believe as big as you can and be willing to take very small steps. Yet that's what 99 percent of people must do to make a difference.

What Do You Believe?

Believing big begins with believing in yourself. Do you believe you can make a difference? Do you believe you have a contribution to make that can positively impact the world? Or are your beliefs about yourself holding you back?

Test it. Take some time to write out all the positive things you can think of about yourself. What do you bring to the table of life? I challenge you to write twenty, fifty, or even one hundred positive things about yourself.

Your One Thing

After you brainstorm and write down the positive potential you bring to this world, take a look at your list. What is your one thing? What is the thing you do better than anything else you do? The authors of *StrengthsFinder*

2.0 say that every person does something better than the next ten thousand people.

What's yours? You may be able to name it instantly, instinctively. If so, great. I hope you're already developing that strength for all it's worth. If not, one of the tasks I encourage you to do before you finish reading this book is to figure out what it is. Look at your personal history. Question your friends and family. Talk to your colleagues. Ask your boss. Take aptitude tests. Do whatever it takes. Until you identify and tap into your one thing, you may find your life going around in circles, and significance will be elusive.

You Are Here!

One of the reasons people don't start small is that they can see a better starting place than where they are. *If I could just be there*, they think, *then starting would be easier.* But the only place anyone can start is where he or she is.

Define where you are and what you have right now. Carrie Rich had a desire to make a difference, lunch money, and an e-mail list. What do you have? Take an inventory. Look at your opportunities. Think about where you currently are. Figure out what's working for and against you. Get the process started.

In the next chapter, I'll prompt you to go deeper inside and tap into what really matters to you. But in the meantime, you need to be willing to get started.

5

Live with a Sense of Anticipation

When is the time to start living out your purpose and experiencing the power of significance? Well, it's *now* of course. But simply saying "take action now" doesn't equip you to make the most of your purpose, does it? So what I want to do is help you to develop the right kind of mindset for performing acts of significance, and the first thing I need to do is guide you to live with a sense of anticipation.

Intentional Anticipation

I've noted that many people want to make a difference when they are confronted with a crisis or tragedy. They will pick up their phones and donate money to Haiti or Japan after a horrific and devastating earthquake. They will donate clothes or supplies for tsunami relief. They will volunteer their time after an unexpected crisis in our country, such as a destructive hurricane or a child abduction.

When urgent things happen, we Americans generally have the heart to respond in that moment, as we did after 9/11. This type of call to perform significant acts occurs every once in a while. While rising to this call is good, and I would certainly encourage you to serve in these kinds of situations, I want to talk about a different kind of urgency in this chapter. It is not a momentary sense of urgency that comes during a crisis. No, this is a kind of urgency that is proactive. It's based on anticipation.

To me, *anticipation* is a wonderfully proactive and intentional word for *seeking out* significance. People with anticipation *plan* to be significant. They *expect* to fulfill their purpose and live a life that matters every day. They *prepare* to do significant acts. They *position* themselves physically, mentally, emotionally, and financially to make a difference in the lives of others. Their sense of anticipation for significance draws them forward.

What does a strong sense of anticipation do for us? It does five things:

1. Anticipation Causes Us to Value Today

Every day I anticipate that I will find an opportunity to do a significant act by adding value to someone. I look at my daily calendar and think about the potential times and places that I can do this. Anticipation causes my mind to look for new significant moments and, when possible, to create them. This has become a discipline of mine. And it can become one of yours.

When you live with intentionality, you *know* and *understand* that every day is your time to make a difference. It's not someday, one day, or maybe tomorrow. It's *today.* You will have the time to make a difference if you want to, so it's about living with the understanding that you can and then taking action.

One specific experience in my life took my sense of anticipation to another level. It happened on the night of our company Christmas party. I had been dancing that night when suddenly I didn't feel very well. One of my team members who was saying good night hugged me, and when she felt the back of my neck, she pointed out that I was in a cold sweat.

I quickly went from feeling bad to worse. Suddenly there was a horrible pain in my chest. I knew I was having a heart attack, so I lay down on the floor as they called for an ambulance.

While I waited, I told everyone how much I loved and appreciated them. I wanted them to know how important they were to me and how valued they were.

When the ambulance arrived, they took me to Grady Hospital in downtown Atlanta. If you're injured with a gunshot or knife wound, Grady is where you want to be.

But not if you're having a heart attack. They didn't have the facility or staff to do the tests I needed for my heart problem. Things did not look good for me.

That was when my assistant, Linda, remembered that six months earlier I had given her the card of a top cardiologist in Nashville. I had met the man when I had lunch with Sam Moore, who was my book publisher at the time. Dr. John Bright Cage had handed me his card and said, "As a doctor, I want to talk to you. You're in trouble. You're overweight and a candidate for a heart attack."

I pretty much dismissed him. I didn't like his message. I told him I handled stress really well and there was nothing to worry about.

"God called me to take care of you," he said. "Take my card, John. Don't lose it, because you are going to need it. And when you do, call me."

I could tell this doctor's intentions were good, so I accepted his card. I didn't give what he said much credence, nor did I value the card. Why would I? I'd recently had a physical and had been told my heart was healthy. Besides, he lived in Nashville—five hours from my home near Atlanta. The likelihood of our paths ever crossing again was relatively small. Despite all this, I gave the card to Linda, and I never gave it another thought.

But Linda sure did. She is the kind of woman who

is always prepared. Back then, before smartphones, she usually carried her Rolodex in the backseat of her car. Thank God she did that night. Her quick thinking and preparation likely saved my life.

Linda called Dr. Cage at 2:00 a.m. to tell him the situation. He knew exactly what needed to be done. It was as if he somehow had been expecting the call. Dr. Cage quickly made arrangements to transfer me to Emory Hospital. Somehow within fifteen minutes, he found a cardiologist to ride in the ambulance with me, without whom I might not have made it. When we arrived at Emory, Dr. Jeff Marshall, the head of cardiology there, and his brilliant team were waiting for me.

"I don't know who you are," said Dr. Marshall greeting the ambulance, "but all four of us were awakened by Dr. Cage to meet you here."

They immediately rolled me into the emergency room.

For a few very long and scary hours, my condition was unstable. When I entered the first hospital, I had three nurses and one doctor watching over me. At Emory a couple of hours later, there were suddenly four of the best doctors in the country overseeing my situation. Although I wasn't clear on everything that was happening, there was one thing I was certain of—*more* doctors in the room was not a good sign.

During this time I was physically very uncomfortable. But *spiritually* I was at peace. Before that incident,

I had often wondered how I would feel when I faced death's door. Now I no longer have to wonder. I was not afraid. You don't really know if you're going to be afraid of death until you've been close enough to touch it, taste it, and smell it. For two and a half hours, I was a hairbreadth from death's door, and yet I was as relaxed and calm as could be.

The only thing I asked of Dr. Marshall that day was to tell me if I was dying.

"You're not dying yet, but if we can't turn this around, you will be," he said.

"Just tell me," I said, fading in and out of consciousness.

Although I had no fear and no regrets, there was one question I kept asking God and myself that fateful night: "Is my purpose complete?" You see, I was only fifty-one. I felt that a person like me couldn't be done! I was too young to have fulfilled my full purpose—my complete *why.* However, as I lay in the hospital bed that night, I knew without a doubt that I had done my best and absolutely could look back upon my life with no regrets about the significance path I had taken. That realization gave me a great deal of peace and comfort.

I will confess to you, I was somewhat surprised I had such peace about my life. The feeling of calm and lack of regret took me aback. If you had given me a phone so that I could take care of any unfinished business, I'm not sure who I would have called. Though I didn't know I was going to have that heart attack, what I found out was that it would become the most amazing spiritual experience of my life. It gave me the greatest confidence in my faith. It proved my faith to me, and I don't question it—ever.

The doctors did pull me through, obviously. Dr. Marshall told me that if I'd had the same heart attack a year earlier, I would have died because the procedure and equipment they used to save me hadn't been available the year before.

After a full recovery, I felt a heightened responsibility to steward my gifts and opportunities. My sense of anticipation was sharpened. I believed strongly that since I was still alive, I probably hadn't totally fulfilled my purpose. There was still more work to do. My purpose is the reason I lived.

Coming out of that experience, here's what I don't know and what I do know.

I don't know when I will die.

I do know that discovering and fulfilling my purpose has allowed me to live my life without regrets.

What about you? If you came to death's door today, would you be facing it without regrets? Do you know why you're here, and have you done your best to fulfill your purpose? If not, you need to find your *why*—the sooner the better. And you need to start living it with a strong sense of anticipation. You must become highly proactive about doing what's significant for you.

My life was forever changed when I had my heart attack, not just because of the physical ramifications or the change in lifestyle I had to make. And not just because of the faith and peace I experienced in the moment I was facing the possibility of my death. What changed? Up until then, I had assumed my days instead of numbering them. The difference between assuming and numbering your days is huge.

Here's what I mean. Until that experience, I always thought I had more time. That day I realized I might not have any more time. I faced the prospect that it might actually be game-over. That realization created a sense of urgency and *anticipation* I had never before felt. It clarified how much I really wanted to make my life count. It was as if God spoke to me and said, "I am not done with you yet. Make the most of the time you have left!"

Nothing lights your fire faster than being given another shot at life. When I survived the heart attack, there was no doubt that I was on a mission. There was a plan much bigger than my own to fulfill and accomplish. I've never looked at life the same since.

I hope you don't have to experience a heart attack to develop the strong sense of anticipation that helps you value today. Whether you know it or not, your days are numbered, just as mine are. But more important, on any given day, when you have a chance to add value to others and perform an act of significance, you may never get that chance again. The moment can pass, and most of the time you don't get that moment back. The opportunity is gone, and the person who could have been helped has gone on his way. That's why you need to seize it.

2. Anticipation Prompts Us to Prepare

Wayne Gretzky is undoubtedly the greatest hockey player ever. I remember hearing him explain in an interview why he was so much more successful than the other hockey players in the game. "Most hockey players follow the puck on the ice," he said. "I never skate to where the puck is. I skate to where it is going." That is a great illustration of anticipation.

Having a strong sense of anticipation changes the way you look at everything, and it makes you prepare differently. For example, every year I search to find the one word that will help me to focus my efforts and attention for the coming year. (I look for just one word because I can't handle a whole sentence!) During that year, I use that word to find many significant lessons and experiences. Identifying this word and using it as a guide has become a discipline for me.

One year the word was *failure*. I decided that every time I was confronted with failure, I would make sure

I understood that it wasn't final by learning from it. It helped me embrace the idea that failed plans should not be interpreted as a failed vision. Plans rarely stay the same, and are scrapped or adjusted as needed. Vision is only refined by failure. It's important to remain stubborn about your vision, but flexible with your plan. Another year I chose the word *success*. Every day I thought, *What is success? Who is successful? Why are they successful? How can I help others be successful?*

When you anticipate that you *can* and *will* make a difference, you prepare differently—for your day, for your year, for your work, for your family, in how you see problems, and in how you see opportunities. Anticipation changes everything.

3. Anticipation Helps Us Generate Good Ideas

When we possess an attitude of anticipation, we expect to come up with good ideas to help us make a difference. Whenever I meet with my team, whether it's to solve a problem, develop a new product or service for one of the companies, or create an initiative to add value to people, we never go into the meeting believing we *won't* come up with good ideas. We expect to succeed. We anticipate positive solutions, and that helps us to come up with them.

How is your attitude when it comes to significance? Do you expect to be able to help other people? Do you anticipate success? Do you believe you will come up with ideas? Do you have enough confidence in your ability to add value that you're willing to share your ideas and solutions? Develop anticipation, and you will start to have more confidence in your ability to make a difference.

4. Anticipation Prompts Us to Look for Ways to Help Others

About twenty years ago I decided I wanted to add value to people with great potential. I started thinking about who, and began with a list of ten people. There were only two criteria. First, I had to be able to add value to them in an area where I knew I could make a substantial impact. Second, they needed to have some success under their belt or be on the cusp of success, and be in need of my help to make a breakthrough. That would ensure that whatever value I added to them would compound. That would make my time and effort like investing in a blue-chip stock where I knew I would get my best return on investment.

In many ways, the ten people I chose were better, faster, and smarter than I was, which was why I wanted to saddle up alongside them, find out what they needed, and give it to them—no questions asked and no conditions.

I very diligently and methodically went after those ten, but I never told them my purpose—unless they asked. In the cases when someone did ask, I'd simply respond by saying, "I want to serve you." But my true desire was to quietly add value to their lives without revealing my reasons.

Doing this sharpened my sense of anticipation, and as I helped them, my belief that I could add value to people only got stronger. The success of others was soon more important to me than my own success. I knew I had experiences and knowledge I could offer to help people. I began to get a bigger thrill watching and celebrating someone else's win than celebrating my own.

Today I still keep a list of the names of ten people I desire to serve. Over the years, the names on the list have changed, though there are a few from that original list that remain. I've served some people for a season and some for a reason. A few I keep serving and plan to serve for a lifetime. I always want to add value to each person on the list. Of course, over time, my goal has grown beyond serving just ten people. But that original list was a catalyst to help me remain intentional in adding value to others, and maintaining that sense of anticipation.

5. Anticipation Helps Us Possess an Abundance Mindset

The previous advantage of anticipation leads to this next one—having an abundance mindset. People live in one of two different kinds of worlds. One world comes from having a scarcity mindset. You cannot give what you do not have. Scarcity thinking has nothing to give. It is preoccupied with receiving. Scarcity thinking is all about me. It says, "There's not enough to go around. I had better get something for myself and hold on to it with all I have." People who live in the world of scarcity think, *There's only one pie, so I'd better get as big a slice as I can before it's all gone.*

People who live in the world of abundance think very differently. They know there's always more. As others scramble and try to grab their slice of pie, people with an abundance mindset think, *That's OK. We'll just bake another pie.*

Abundance thinking is the mindset of people of significance, and it has nothing to do with how much they have. They may not have financial wealth. They may not live in great situations. But whatever they have, they are willing to share because they don't worry about running out. They can be their brother's keepers, because they believe there is more to be found, more to be created. If there isn't a way now, another one will be invented.

What may surprise you is that two people who occupy the same space, face the exact same circumstances, and receive the same opportunities can live in these two different worlds. One person can be restricted by thinking in terms of scarcity. The other can have an abundance mindset that makes nearly anything possible. Their thinking, more than almost anything else, has an impact on whether they live as haves or have-nots.

When I talk to people about abundance and scarcity mindsets, I sometimes ask, "Which would you *prefer* to have?" Everybody raises their hand for abundance, yet many struggle because they are mentally stuck in the scarcity world.

So I'll ask you the question: Which world would you prefer to live in, scarcity or abundance? If having an abundance mindset is difficult for you, the good news is that you can change. You can use *anticipation* to help you change the way you think and act. How? By practicing positive anticipation for yourself and others. Anticipation is a key that unlocks the doors to abundance thinking.

"Doors?" you may be asking. "Don't you mean *door*?"

No. Expecting there to be only one door is scarcity thinking.

Let me explain how anticipation begins and grows in your life.

There is a door of opportunity before you. Maybe you see it; maybe you don't. But it is there. If you have positive anticipation, you assume it's there, and you make the effort to find it, and if you are diligent in that effort, you will find it. But know this. It may be locked, and it may require a lot of effort for you to unlock it and walk through it. Are you willing to give it a try? *Do you believe you can?* Some people will try and some people won't. I hope you're someone who's willing.

What usually makes the difference? Anticipation. When you have positive anticipation, you believe that you can open the door. And if you anticipate that something positive could be on the other side, you will try to open it.

So let's say you are willing. You do have positive anticipation, which, by the way, is a choice, because we don't know what will be behind that door. If you walk through that door, do you know what you will find? More doors. There is not one door of opportunity. There is not one door to significance. There is a series of doors. What keeps you moving forward, unlocking those doors? Anticipation!

Finding and going through one door is an event. Going through many doors is a lifestyle. That requires an abundance mindset. Every time you open another door, your anticipation gets stronger and is validated. Over time, it can become part of your DNA. And if you keep going through doors, you will create success, and you will have a chance to achieve significance. You will make a difference. It's almost inevitable.

Sadly, too many people have a scarcity mindset and lack positive anticipation. As a result, they never open the first door. Unopened doors reinforce scarcity thinking and scarcity living. Others do open that first door, but when it doesn't offer what they expected, they become disappointed and abandon the pursuit. They give up.

Don't let that happen to you. Don't let the gap between expectation and reality disappoint you. Don't let it kill your sense of anticipation. Keep searching for doors and opening them. And remember that with each open door, your anticipation will increase and so will abundance.

If you find this difficult, then begin changing your thinking by recalling your past successes and keeping them in the forefront of your mind. Think about risks you took that led to rewards. Think about opportunities you pursued that gave you success. Think about the lessons you learned even when things didn't go your way, and how you later benefited from those lessons. Rely on these memories. They can give you a frame of reference to anticipate good things happening in your future. If you anticipate the positives and couple that with a desire to help and add value to others, you can make a difference.

Building a House of Significance

The journey of positive anticipation that I just shared with you has been a reality in my life. To me, living a life that matters is like building a house. The process started with wanting to make a difference in the lives of others. Once I went through that first doorway, I entered my first room of significance. And I discovered some wonderful ways that I could make a difference in the lives of others.

Each day that I lived in that room, I intentionally tried to add value to someone. Some days were better than others, but each day was an intentional effort to help someone. I experienced more wins than losses, and each time I added value to someone, it added value to me. My intentional sowing resulted in eventual reaping. Out of my sense of abundance, I looked for more significance. Anticipation fed my desire to do more.

With each day, making a difference unlocked another door. I was starting to make a difference in the lives of more people. When the second door opened, it allowed me to live in two rooms. That second room allowed me to discover my strengths, the things I could do better than anything else. Those strengths included leading, communicating, and connecting. As I practiced those strengths, my significance became more focused and that laser concentration began bringing a higher return. It was in this room that I found my purpose, my *why*. Knowing my reason for existence empowered me to become more strategic about everything, but above all else in the area of significance. What more could I do to make a difference?

My anticipation fed my questioning until I found an answer that caused me to search for the third door in my significance journey. With anticipation, I unlocked the third door, which is fulfilling my purpose while working with other like-minded people. This new room was filled with people who were potential partners in significance. I'm grateful for this because of my personal limitations. Alone I can only do so much. The compounding potential and return of working with others makes my sense of anticipation soar.

During the first few years I was in this room, I constantly looked for people who could add value to me. This limited me and the significance I could achieve. But then I realized that I should be focusing on adding value to the people who partnered with me. Today, as I live in this area, I have one desire: to find people who are like-minded and like-valued so that I can lift them and their levels of significance.

For many years, my house of significance only had three rooms. It seemed to me that my dream house was finished. Yet the longer I connected with others and worked with them and served them, the clearer it became that they had a desire to transform individuals, communities, and even countries. Soon I was identifying transformational leaders and the qualities they possess.

I watched them and followed them and they led me to another door of opportunity: intentionality. These leaders embrace intentional living. They live with anticipation and seize opportunities to make a difference. They live with an urgency that empowers them to make each day a masterpiece of significance. Their intensity and focus cannot be denied. They anticipate the needs of others. Their behavior backs up their beliefs, and their actions underscore and build more anticipation. They are living the significance cycle: anticipation, action, abundance, anticipation, action, abundance. When I understood this and partnered with others, we were able to make a difference together at a whole new level.

If you possess an abundance mindset, this probably makes sense to you. Fantastic! Don't hesitate. Move forward.

If you have a scarcity mindset, it may be harder for you to live with positive anticipation. If you want to change, consider this. If you live with a scarcity mindset, you will get what you expect. You will have scarcity. Guaranteed. No one experiences abundance while anticipating scarcity. So why not try on abundance? At best, you'll experience abundance. At worst, you'll get the scarcity you've already been experiencing. You have nothing to lose. Believe, anticipate, take action, give, and see what happens. It could change your life.

Undoubtedly, this is also your time to make a difference. If you live with positive anticipation, you can do it. Maybe you are already doing it. Or maybe you're in the preparation stages—searching for the first door of opportunity, or for the second or third door. Where you are in the process doesn't matter. As long as you are engaged in it and anticipate positive results, you're on your way. The only thing left for you to do is understand how to seize opportunities to make a difference. And that is the subject of the final chapter of this book.

Significant Application:
Live with a Sense of Anticipation

Anticipating Today's Impact

When you woke up this morning, what was your mind-set related to making a difference? Did you *believe* you could make a difference? Did you *expect* to make a difference? Or did you even think about it at all?

What can you do to ratchet up your sense of antici-pation every day? How can you remind yourself to make this a part of your everyday existence? What can you do to remind yourself that *now* is the time to find ways to help and add value to people? Perhaps you need to put a Post-it note on your bathroom mirror or computer screen. Maybe you need to pin up a photo-graph of someone you helped in the past so that you see it every day and are inspired to take action. Maybe you need to make a message of anticipation your home screen on your phone or computer desktop. Maybe you need a daily reminder sent to you on your phone at an opportune time. Or maybe you can ask someone to hold you accountable for taking action every day or week.

Do whatever is necessary to help you develop a sense of positive anticipation for making a difference.

Get Ready

In what ways are you preparing to make a difference? My old mentor John Wooden used to say, "When opportunity comes, it's too late to prepare." Are you preparing? Are you anticipating your chance to make a difference? When you get that chance, will you be ready?

I suggest that you do two things to help you be ready. First, gather your resources. Think about what you have that you can use to help others. Second, create margins in your life. Many people fail to make a difference because they are so busy. They move so fast that they don't see the opportunities, or they have so much to do that they believe they don't have the time to stop and help. Don't be one of those people!

Do You Believe in Abundance?

Which are you: a scarcity person or an abundance person? If you're not an abundance person, follow the advice in this chapter. Look to your past for inspiration. Make a list of your past successes. Add to that list every advantage, gift, or benefit you've ever received that you did not earn. Add to the list the positive lessons you've learned from your mistakes and failures.

If you give this exercise the time it deserves, you'll come up with a very long list. In fact, if you keep the list handy during the next several days, weeks, or month, you might be able to surprise yourself with how many positive things you come up with.

Now here's the point. Look at the list. If scarcity is the norm, how in the world have you experienced so many positive things? Abundance is out there. You just need to believe in it and anticipate that you will benefit from it. Make the mental shift to abundance. And whenever you are tempted to feel discouraged or cynical, pull out that long list and review it again.

6

Seize Significance Opportunities Every Day

In November of 1989, I was standing in the kitchen of our home in San Diego when I heard on the news that the Berlin Wall was being torn down. It was clear to me that without a doubt, history was being made that very moment. I was headed to my home office, but I turned to Margaret and said, "We need to go there. I think we should get the kids on a plane and go now. They've got to see this."

Then I went to my office, as I usually did each morning, because there were a couple of things on my schedule that needed my attention.

I got absorbed in my work and within minutes, the urgency of trying to get to Berlin faded. I thought, *Berlin can wait*. And the moment slipped away.

Forever.

I have always felt frustration over that decision.

Going to Berlin with my kids to see the wall come down was a once-in-a-lifetime opportunity. It would have been worth the time, money, and difficulty to get there. I wanted to show my kids what can happen to a country when leadership goes bad. Because of the division of Berlin after World War II, families got separated. Then the East Germans made their own people prisoners by putting up a wall. That wall was a symbol of evil and corrupt leadership. And its destruction was a symbol of hope and positive leadership, not by a government but by the people.

I wanted my children to see that it was ordinary people who were taking down the wall. They had come to a place where they said, "No more." I wanted my kids to experience the celebration and joy of the moment. And I wanted them to have a piece of the wall as a reminder of this powerful event in history.

Even with all those reasons to go, I didn't act. I lost my sense of urgency. And as a result, I missed a chance to give them a moment we could all share that would have had a long-lasting impact on their lives.

There are times in life when you have to seize an opportunity to make an experience meaningful and to bring the important people in your life into an environment of significance. If you don't anticipate the opportunity, recognize that something is happening, and seize that moment, you can miss those rare occurrences that really matter. I had the time and resources to make the trip to Berlin happen. But I didn't act with intentionality.

Have you ever done that? Have you ever had an idea to do something that could make a difference in the life of another person, yet you let it slip away because you lacked a sense of *urgency*? I have to admit, that's happened too many times in my life. I wish I could seize every opportunity that came my way. I know that's unrealistic, but it's my desire just the same.

In our harried and busy lives, is there ever a *convenient* time to make a difference? Probably not. Is there ever a *right* time? Yes. *It's now—when we see the opportunity!* How do we help ourselves to become more action oriented? We maintain a sense of urgency for seizing significance opportunities every day.

Adopting the Right Mindset to Seize Opportunities

I believe every generation gets an opportunity to make a difference, but the people of that generation have to *seize* that opportunity. When Bobby Kennedy was assassinated in 1968, I remember sitting in my living room, reading in the newspaper a quote that was often associated with him and his brother President John F. Kennedy. "There are those that look at things as they are and ask, 'Why?' I dream of things that never were and ask, 'Why not?' "

I was a junior in college in 1968, and this was a

defining time for me. There was something about that quote that grabbed me. I understood exactly what Kennedy was saying. And I related to it. I discovered that I was not someone who quit because of obstacles or who would be stopped when others wanted to question *why* something new should be done. I was definitely a possibilities person. I was fearless in my willingness to question what I didn't know—to challenge others with new ways of thinking and doing things. I knew right then I was going to be a person who walked through life asking, "Why not?" I believed in my ability to change things for the better. From that day forward, I tried to seize opportunities and find ways to make things happen.

My journey of significance has been progressive, but it has always been rooted in the desire to act now. I don't wait for tomorrow, next week, next month, next year, or someday when I can get around to taking action. I always focus on *today*. And my sense of urgency has grown as I've gotten older. My significance journey started small but it multiplied as my capability to see bigger developed. It's still developing, and I hope to keep repeating the cycle of growth, with what I do getting bigger and better. But that improvement depends on taking action, on seizing opportunities as they come.

Let me say something about opportunities. They do not multiply because they are *seen*. Many people see opportunities. Opportunities multiply because they are *seized.* And the more people seize opportunities, the more they see them. It becomes a positive cycle. That's why we need to live with a sense of urgency.

The saying "you can make a difference at any time, but the best time is now" drives people who possess anticipation and live with intentionality. There is no time like the present. Tomorrow is not guaranteed. Yesterday is too late. Living with purpose means always thinking, "There's something more I can do." As poet Ralph Waldo Emerson said, "You cannot do a calling too soon for you never know how soon it will be too late."

Five Ways to Seize Opportunities

As you step forward into the power of significance by embracing your purpose, you must train yourself to anticipate and seize opportunities. Urgency must become part of your mindset. It must become a lifestyle. If you want to live a great story by making a difference, are willing to start small, have passion, know your *why*, put others first, add value to people from your sweet spot, and live with a sense of anticipation, there's only one thing left for you to do to make a difference: seize opportunities.

It will be difficult for me to coach you on the specifics of seizing opportunities, because every person, every situation, and every day is different. But I can show you several places where every person has a chance to seize opportunities to make a difference. You can make a significance impact in the following ways:

1. Be the First to Help Someone

I want to ask you to do something. Think about three people who were the first to step up and be there for you at some point in your life when you had a crisis, problem, or dire need. Who helped you when you really needed it?

What was the difficulty you had?

Who was it that stepped forward to help? Write down their names.

What did they do?

OK, now I want you to think really hard for this next question. In that situation, who was the *second* person to help you?

I bet you can't remember, can you? If I offered you a million dollars, you probably couldn't write down that person's name.

Why? The people who most often make the biggest difference are the people who are first to step up and help at a time when it makes a difference.

This has been true in my life. I remember the people who made a difference first.

- They set themselves apart from all of the others.
- They will always have a special place in my heart.

- They planted the first seeds of success in my life.
- Their seeds compounded into a bountiful harvest of significant living!

When you receive the kind of support and belief that I have, there is tremendous motivation and desire to provide that type of inspiration to other people too. Every morning that I am booked to speak to a group, I wake up with great anticipation because I believe I am going to make a difference in people's lives that day.

It never fails to happen to me: my expectation, eagerness, and anticipation are off the charts. By the time I get to the venue, I am almost kid-like with excitement. As I am teaching, I am filled with great joy because I know, without a doubt, I am giving the group something that will work and has the potential to transform their lives. I understand the impact the information I am handing over can have if they take action. I know what's possible if they seize the opportunity.

Are you on the lookout for opportunities where you can be the first to help people? The first to encourage them? The first to open doors that they cannot open on their own? Do you have a sense of urgency? Look around. Maybe you can be the first to encourage a member of your family. Maybe you can help someone you're ahead of at work to solve a problem, acquire a skill, or benefit from your experience. Maybe you can come to the aid of a neighbor or a stranger. The opportunities are there. You just need to open your eyes, recognize them, and *seize* them.

2. Take a Risk When the Potential for Significance Is High

What opportunities to make a difference do you see that you know hold risks? How do you know when the risk is worth the effort? How do you know the timing is right? These are tough questions. You can do what I often do and make a list of the pros and cons and weigh them against one another. You can do a risk analysis where you chart the probability against the consequences. If you're a person of faith, you can pray.

The process is different for everybody. But let me say this: Don't ever dismiss an opportunity just because it has risks—because everything has risks. You could fear risk so much that you decide never to leave the safety of your home...yet you could still die if a tree fell on your bedroom while you slept or your house caught fire. If you're going to have a bias in a direction, have a bias toward action. In the end, people most often regret the chances they *failed* to take, not the chances they took that failed.

3. Do What You Know Is Right, Even with No Promise of Return

We often tend to judge opportunities by the potential return. There's nothing wrong with that. In fact, I encourage you to be strategic in your thinking. However, there are also times when we are faced with opportunities to do things that we know are right, even if we don't know where they will lead or what the result will be.

I want to encourage you to follow through and seize these kinds of opportunities, because the return on giving is always higher than what we give. I'm still surprised by the impact a simple act can have on someone, but I am never surprised by the outcome of intentional living.

Whenever I write a book or record a CD, I believe it will help someone. I don't always know who, when, or where, but I know without a doubt that it will have a significant impact, and that's what keeps me motivated to keep seizing these kinds of opportunities. And that's why I do it.

And that's why you should perform intentional acts of significance. If you maintain a sense of urgency and obey your instinct to do the right thing, especially when it plays to your strengths, it may have a greater impact than you would ever dream. I embrace the words of the apostle Paul, who advised, "So let's not allow ourselves to get fatigued doing good. At the right time we will harvest a good crop if we don't give up, or quit. Right now, therefore, every time we get the chance, let us work for the benefit of all."[4] Even if you aren't a person of faith, you can embrace these words because you probably instinctively know that you reap what you sow.

4. Give to Your Peers at a Time When It Makes a Difference

I had the opportunity to connect with Condoleezza Rice a few years ago, and I found out she was teaching freshmen at Stanford University. I was curious about what motivated her to return to teaching after her career in Washington was done. After all, she had been to the highest peak, sitting in the most influential meetings in the world with incredible people, listening and participating in the most intense and purposeful discussions. She had been a part of the world's most powerful think tanks. And yet, now, she was back in the classroom. I wanted to know if this was something she planned to do for a year or two and then move on, or if she was looking at a longer-term commitment. Condoleezza explained that her decision to teach was deliberate and full of intention:

> The classroom is the molder of the opinion of the lives of people. I came back because if I can change a nineteen-year-old's life, that is much more significant than what I was doing, because I get them on the front end.

I loved her answer and the notion of impacting people on the front end of their lives, especially young people who have great potential and just need someone, like a teacher, a coach, or a boss, to come along and believe in them.

I like to think of myself as a lid-lifter in people's lives. I love to find people I believe in and in whom I see great potential, and come into their lives through what I teach or through words of encouragement to follow their dreams of significance. But I have benefited from the help of others even more than I've helped others. Many people have added value to me. For example, when I had my heart attack, my friend Jack Hayford, who is an author and a pastor, called me and said he'd handle any and all requests for speaking engagements for the next six months for me so I could recover, focus on my health, and get stronger. He stepped in at a time that really mattered to me. He understood that I would have a hard time saying no to the invitations, so he offered to say yes for me and take my place. What a great friendship and blessing in my life that allowed me to recover.

How can you come alongside a peer and help him or her? What opportunities are presenting themselves right now? Not someday. Not when it's more convenient. Right now. Who could you give a leg up? I guarantee there's somebody in your life who could use your help and who would be forever grateful.

5. Plant the Seeds of Intentionality in Children

One of the most important things we can do is pass along to the next generation what we've learned. I do that every day as I train leaders, develop my team, and speak to people on personal growth. But the place where it's most important to me is close to home. Margaret and I planted the seeds of our values in our children, and now we are doing it with our grandchildren. And one of the most important seeds we plant is intentionality.

When we are young, the books our parents read to us have the power to imprint values upon us and encourage us, even at the youngest age. Early reading is how many children learn life's basics, including colors, numbers, letters, and stories. So much of the information that we store in our brains as we grow older and mature is put there in our early years.

I love the books of Dr. Seuss. He was very clever in placing intentional messages of significance within his books, and those seeds have been planted in millions of children at an early age. His writing has been taught in classrooms for years because of the simple yet poignant nature of his messages. If we shared Dr. Seuss's message with every child, it would have the power to impact and change the world. Here's what I mean. Look at lines such as these:

"Unless someone like you cares a whole awful lot, nothing is going to get better. It's not."[5]

"You have brains in your head. You have feet in your shoes. You can steer yourself in any direction you choose."[6]

"You're off to great places! Today is your day! Your mountain is waiting! So get on your way!"[7]

Though each of these lines comes within the context of a story, it communicates an important life lesson that can never be given too early to kids. The sooner they understand the value of living with intentionality, the more quickly they can start living lives of significance. What we teach our children to love and appreciate is far more important than what we teach them to know.

As a result of my parents being so intentional with me, I became an extremely intentional parent with my own children. Thankfully, Margaret and I saw eye to eye on this need in our child-rearing years, and our kids reaped the benefits of our actions.

Margaret intentionally took the kids to school every morning. She never let them take the bus because she wanted the last words they would hear before they went off to class each day to be positive ones from her. She was also purposely at home when they were done with classes and their extracurricular activities. Margaret was always making sure they had a comfortable place to sit and tell her about their day. Not everyone can do that, but if you could, why wouldn't you?

Today, my grandchildren also reap the benefits of the intentionality my parents instilled in me as a child, though their methods of retaining the lessons we teach tend to be a bit more high tech than mine were. My granddaughter Maddie keeps a running list of principles either her dad (my son-in-law, Steve) or I teach her. She also records poignant lines she reads from some of my books. She keeps all these things in her iPhone. Every time she comes across a new quote, she adds it to her "Daddy/Papa List."

Recently I asked her to share with me some of the things she has captured. Here are a few of them:

- Attitude is a choice.
- Maturity is seeing things from another person's point of view and being flexible.
- Always plan ahead. You're either prepared or repaired.
- You are what you do every day.
- Failure is inevitable, but learning is optional.

Having a list like this helps Maddie value herself and build her self-esteem. Sometimes she and I will talk about one of the quotes on her list so that I can reinforce that principle or lesson. I prefer talking to her in person whenever possible, though as a teenager, she likes to text. I don't want to lose the opportunity to strengthen her intentionality, so I will send her reminders and follow up with her to make sure we are always in touch. It's a really great way for me to be connected to my granddaughter, something I appreciate and I know she does too.

Margaret and I are even intentional at Christmas. Our gift to our children and grandchildren every year is a trip. We want to have wonderful experiences together while we can. During these trips, each member of our family knows that I will ask them two questions: "What did you love, and what did you learn?"

I asked this when my children were young, and I still ask it. Why? Because our best teacher isn't experience. It's evaluated experience. Answering those questions prompts them to evaluate what they've experienced. We are intentional in making sure that each experience becomes a lesson that can be learned and understood for their personal development.

Our family tradition at Christmas is to give the first gift to Jesus since it is his birthday. All year long, our grandchildren put aside money in their Jesus bank. Then on Christmas Eve, they give the first gift to the charity of their choice.

Don't miss your opportunity to pour intentionality into the lives of your children or grandchildren. It is never too early to start. If you can create a significance mindset in them when they are young, you don't have to try to create it later in life. They won't have to break old habits or create new ones to start living a life that matters. They will already have those habits.

Having the courage and responsibility to instill intentionality in our children can change the way they live. The possibilities are boundless and the timing critical. You have to possess a sense of urgency in this area because the time we have with our children and grandchildren is really very short.

My dream is to raise up a generation of intentional people. It may not be this generation, or even the next one. But if the next generation has the seeds planted early on and then believes in the power of intentionality, imagine the impact they could have on the world they live in.

Living with Significance Every Day

My greatest hope is that people everywhere will become intentional in seizing opportunities to make a difference to transform their families, businesses, neighborhoods, communities, cities, and countries. I believe that when we tap into the power of significance and embrace purpose, we can change the world and make it a better place.

Author and speaker Jim Collins says, "Transformation

can only happen if you have transformational leaders." Jim has studied transformational leadership culture more than anyone else has, so I believe he's right. That's why I'm working so hard right now to help others live intentionally and influence others for positive change.

Recently I met a transformational leader whose story inspires me to keep trying to make a difference, and I believe his story will also inspire you. His name is Jeff Williams. He is an independent business owner who has embraced significance and is living his purpose every day.

Jeff's journey to significance began when he was only eight years old. He grew up in a family of very modest means. They didn't have much. They got by, but there were no extras. Jeff says that on the rare occasion that they went to McDonald's, his parents would buy him a burger, but he'd never get the fries or a drink. That's how tight things were at home for him growing up.

One day a salesman in a suit showed up at Jeff's house with a sample case full of books called *Uncle Arthur's Bedtime Stories*. Jeff remembers peeking around the edge of the dining room doorway hearing the salesman's pitch to his parents in their living room. "These books are so well made," the salesman said, "a child can make a mess with peanut butter and jam, and it will wipe right off."

That's what I eat for lunch! Jeff thought as he listened.

Jeff was shocked when his parents splurged and bought a set of the books.

It was a life-changing opportunity.

Every night Jeff's mom or dad would read him one of the stories. Jeff loved them so much, he would sometimes stay up late and read ahead.

One night Jeff's parents read a story that would change his life. To this day he remembers it vividly. It was called "Wilfred's Secret." It was the story of a boy and his sister who decided to create what they called "The Surprise Package Company," where they secretly left gifts for sick kids laid up in bed or anonymously gave food to shut-in old ladies.

The story inspired Jeff right down to his soul. "Something just ignited on the inside of me," says Jeff. "Doing that would be so cool, to be a blessing to other people and surprise people. And for me the great thrill was watching them discover the surprise without their knowing I was there. And to see the delight in their eyes."

So Jeff enlisted the aid of his sister, and they started doing what the brother and sister in the story did. They gave away some of their toys and made crafts, which they gave to people anonymously. "That was the seed of generosity that God has gifted me with," says Jeff.

Jeff's life turned upside down just a few years after that, and his family life turned, in Jeff's words, "crazy." But the desire to make a difference was already inside of him.

Flash forward more than a decade, and Jeff, though young, was married and had four children. He worked in the restaurant business and then in direct marketing. They didn't have much, but they were always givers.

Jeff remembers a young couple who had worked with them in direct marketing, but had then left the business. They were struggling. Jeff and his family bought a bunch of groceries for them. He and the kids put the groceries on their doorstep, then hid in bushes around the corner as a stranger they recruited rang the couple's doorbell. Secretly watching their reaction and knowing they had made a difference made him and his kids feel good.

Jeff experienced modest success in direct marketing, but the thing that had most inspired him was the realization that if he made a lot of money, he could give a lot away. And that became his dream. Soon he started his own company. After years of hard work, the company began to be successful.

By the time I met Jeff, he was already making a difference in the lives of others. When I traveled to Guatemala in 2013 to teach values in roundtables, he traveled with us. There he met a man named Carlos who was taking care of orphans and saving malnourished children from starvation. Jeff recognized that Carlos was a like-valued person, and they began partnering together to make a difference. Jeff has funded the building of a small village for orphans with Carlos in Guatemala.

And every month, Jeff pays to send some of his employees and their families to Guatemala to serve there.

Jeff has also come alongside me, and we are partnering together to make a difference. Jeff has helped me and the nonprofit John Maxwell Leadership Foundation to develop a transformational effort in the seven streams of influence: arts, entertainment, sports, and culture; business; education; family; faith; government; and media.

One of the things I love most about Jeff is that he is just as intentional and entrepreneurial about making a difference as he is about developing his business. He lives each day with a strong sense of urgency for significance. And the gains he makes in the marketplace are being put to greater use to serve others.

"The other day I came up with this business idea," said Jeff, "and I got so excited because immediately I thought, *Wow, this is going to be successful. It's going to make my company more successful, and now I can give away extra money next October. Where do I want to give that?*"

What Jeff is living is also being passed on to his children. Recently, he learned that when his daughter Deanna was twelve, she quietly and secretly saved her allowance and other money to sponsor seven underprivileged children at a summer horse camp that Jeff and his family worked with. At $225 per child, that means Deanna had given more than $1,500!

Jeff knows and lives his purpose. Always intentional, he is actively looking for ways to make a difference on a continual basis. And I love his big-picture goal the most. "I hope one day to use my story to challenge a thousand other businesspeople to do the same thing: to pick a project, get involved, fund it, and get their staff involved, too." Now, that's significance. If everybody thought like Jeff and had his sense of urgency, the world would change in no time.

When you live a life of purpose, you wake up anticipating that you will make a positive impact on people's lives every day. You look for opportunities everywhere, and when you see one that taps into your *why* and adds value from your sweet spot, you seize it. Jeff does that every day. So do I. *So can you!* All you have to do is possess a sense of urgency and seize the moment. It doesn't have to be big. It doesn't have to be earth-shattering. It just needs to be for others. If we can do it, so can you. You can taste significance, and once you've tasted significance, anything less will never satisfy you again.

Significant Application:
Seize Significance Opportunities
Every Day

Become an Entrepreneur for Significance

I love spending time with business entrepreneurs. I love their creativity, their work ethic, their sense of urgency, and their willingness to risk. But as much as I enjoy spending time with them, I love being with significance entrepreneurs even more. These are people who...

- See things that unintentional people do not see.
- Believe things that unintentional people do not believe.
- Feel things that unintentional people do not feel.
- Say things that unintentional people do not say.
- Do things that unintentional people do not do.

Take a look at those five phrases and write about each of them. What opportunities do you see that others don't? What do you believe and feel about them? What are you willing to say that others are afraid to say about them? What are you willing to do? Put together all of those ideas to write a manifesto of intentional significance that you can live by.

Be More Intentional Helping Children

I believe it is impossible to be too intentional in helping children. If you're a parent or grandparent, start with the children in your family. If they're young enough, read to them. If I could do only one thing to help the children of the world, it would be to teach them to read well. A person who can read can learn to do anything else.

Become intentional about everything you do with your children. Talk to them continually to encourage them. Teach them in any way you can, including on vacations. Model good values. Help them to reach their potential.

If you don't have children of your own, help a younger sibling. Spend time with a niece or nephew. Volunteer at a school. Offer to mentor a young person. Find a way to add value to people of the next generation, especially from your sweet spot. An investment in them is an investment in significance.

Who Needs Help?

Who among your peers could use a hand? See that as an opportunity to add value and seize it as an avenue into significant living. If you give with no expectation of return, you can make a difference and live a life that matters.

EPILOGUE

Share Your Significance Story

I'm currently seventy years old. People sometimes ask me why I don't slow down. "Why are you pressing?" they ask. Because my age tells me that my time is limited. I'm reminded of the words of King David of ancient Israel, who wrote, "Teach me O Lord about the end of my life. Teach me about the number of my days I have left so I may know how temporary my life is."[8]

I know my time is limited. I want my life to matter. I want to fulfill my purpose. I want to be significant. I know that I need to live with intentionality and a sense of urgency. If I want to make a difference, I need to do it *now*.

What about you? Do you have a sense of urgency for fulfilling your purpose and embracing significance? You may be younger than I am and feel you have plenty of time left.

Do you?

If you start now—today—then the answer is yes. You still have time to do something significant. Why? Because significance is not a *destination* thing—it's a *daily* thing. As my mentor John Wooden used to say, "Make every day your masterpiece." Significance is not about someday; it's about today. You can make a difference anytime—but the best time is *now*.

A Life with No Regrets

I once asked Coach John Wooden if he had any regrets about decisions he had made throughout his life.

"I have none," he said.

His answer shocked me.

"*None?*" I asked.

"I made every decision with a pure heart, the right heart. If you asked me if all of my decisions were good, I'd tell you they weren't. But you didn't ask me that. You asked if I regret any."

I looked at him with great wonder and admiration. Surely, I have not known many people throughout my life who could have given me this same answer with such confidence. In fact, at the time he said it, I could not think of any!

"You see, John, I did the very best that I could at that time to make each decision. Is there anything else you can expect from yourself?"

That conversation had a profound impact on me. I wish I had made every decision with good motives, but I can't say with integrity that I always have. I've done more than my share of dumb things. I've made mistakes. I've had wrong motives. I'm not trying to hold myself up as a model. Still, I don't want to go through life with regret—not for any reason. Even when I have made mistakes along the way, I've used those experiences to learn and grow. They've made me stronger, smarter, and more thoughtful along the way. I want you to learn from my mistakes, just as I have. Maybe I can save you a few steps.

You see, we all go through life doing the best we can. We can't legitimately offer more than we know. We can't perform at a higher level than our experiences have taught us to or come to a greater place than our expertise has brought us to. However, once you have opened yourself up to something new—to the possibility of what can be—it's hard to ignore the potential you see. At least, it always has been that way for me.

You can try, but ultimately, you really can't unlearn what you know. Sure, you can choose not to practice it. You can stash it away, push it to the back of your memory bank, and pretend it doesn't exist. But once the information has traveled into the portals of your mind, it's there, it's ready, and it's calling for action. What you do with that information is up to you. Whether you practice the principle you know to be true is simply a choice. And it's yours alone to make.

What Will Your Decision Be?

Now you know how to live a life of purpose. You know that significance is within your reach. You know what it means to be intentional. So I want to ask you a series of questions. See how many you can honestly answer yes to:

- ❏ Are you choosing to live a story of significance?
- ❏ Are you actively searching for your why so that you can make a difference?
- ❏ Are you choosing to live with intentionality, not just good intentions?
- ❏ Are you willing to start small but believe big to make a difference?
- ❏ Are you living with a sense of anticipation for making a difference?
- ❏ Are you seizing opportunities and taking action to make a difference?

If you answered yes to all of these questions—or if you are willing to answer yes and take action *now*—then you have crossed over into the significant life. You are tapping into the power of significance, and you will make a difference. Your life will matter. You will start to change the world because you've made the right decision. Now you just need to manage that decision every day of your life. You just need to keep living with purpose and taking action in some small way every day.

What's Your Story?

If you have crossed over, I want to hear about it. I want to know your story of significance. I want you to tell me and others about how you seized an opportunity to make a difference and took action. It can be small or big. It can be your first or your best. It can be a story of heart or hope, humor or help. It can be a paragraph, a poem, a series of photos, or a video. The only important thing is that it's *your* story.

I've even created a place for you to tell it. It's a website called **MyIntentionalLivingStory.com**. Go there and tell the world how you're making a difference. My dream is to help one million people become intentional, start making a difference, and tell their stories. I want you to be a part of that.

If you join me in my dream of making a difference, together maybe we can start a movement—a movement toward a world full of purpose and significance, where people think of others before themselves, where adding value to others is a priority, where financial gain is second to future potential, and where people's self-worth is strengthened by acts of significance every day.

If we each live a life that truly matters, we can change the world. Until then, I want to leave you with these words from a Franciscan blessing:

May God bless you with discomfort,
At easy answers, half-truths,
And superficial relationships
So that you may live
Deep within your heart.

May God bless you with anger
At injustice, oppression,
And exploitation of people,
So that you may work for
Justice, freedom, and peace.

May God bless you with tears,
To shed for those who suffer pain,
Rejection, hunger, and war,
So that you may reach out your hand
To comfort them and
To turn their pain to joy

And may God bless you
With enough foolishness
To believe that you can
Make a difference in the world,

So that you can do
What others claim cannot be done
To bring justice and kindness
To all our children and the poor.
Amen.[9]

Notes

1. Donald Miller, *A Million Miles in a Thousand Years: What I Learned While Editing My Life* (Nashville: Thomas Nelson, 2009), 59–60.
2. Kevin Hall, *Aspire: Discovering Your Purpose through the Power of Words* (New York: William Morrow, 2010), 58.
3. Proverbs 18:21, MSG.
4. Galatians 6:9–10, MSG.
5. Dr. Seuss, *The Lorax* (New York: Random House, 1971).
6. Dr. Seuss, *Oh, the Places You'll Go!* (New York: Random House, 1960).
7. Ibid.
8. Psalm 39:4, GW.
9. "A Franciscan Blessing," Franciscans Na Proinnsiasaigh Irish Franciscans OFM [website], http://www.franciscans.ie/news/83 -news-scroller/485-a-franciscan-blessing, accessed December 13, 2014.

About the Author

John C. Maxwell is a #1 *New York Times* bestselling author, coach, and speaker who has sold more than twenty-six million books in fifty languages. In 2014 he was identified as the #1 leader in business by the American Management Association® and the most influential leadership expert in the world by *Business Insider* and *Inc.* magazine. He is the founder of The John Maxwell Company, The John Maxwell Team, EQUIP, and The John Maxwell Leadership Foundation, organizations that have trained millions of leaders. In 2015 they reached the milestone of having trained leaders from every country of the world. The recipient of the Mother Teresa Prize for Global Peace and Leadership from the Luminary Leadership Network, Dr. Maxwell speaks each year to Fortune 500 companies, presidents of nations, and many of the world's top business leaders. He can be followed at Twitter.com/JohnCMaxwell. For more information about him, visit JohnMaxwell.com.

John Maxwell's Bestselling Successful People Series—More Than One Million Copies Sold

WHAT SUCCESSFUL PEOPLE KNOW ABOUT LEADERSHIP

Advice from America's #1 Leadership Authority

The best leaders strive constantly to learn and grow, and every leader faces challenges. Discover actionable advice and solutions, as John Maxwell answers the most common leadership questions he receives.

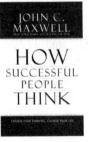

HOW SUCCESSFUL PEOPLE THINK

Change Your Thinking, Change Your Life

Good thinkers are always in demand. They solve problems, never lack ideas, and always have hope for a better future. In this compact read, Maxwell reveals eleven types of successful thinking, and how you can maximize each to revolutionize your work and life.

HOW SUCCESSFUL PEOPLE LEAD

Taking Your Influence to the Next Level

True leadership is not generated by your title. In fact, being named to a position is the lowest of the five levels every effective leader achieves. Learn how to be more than a boss people are required to follow, and extend your influence beyond your immediate reach for the benefit of others.

HOW SUCCESSFUL
PEOPLE GROW

15 Ways to Get Ahead in Life

John Maxwell explores the principles that are proven to be the most effective catalysts for personal growth. You can learn what it takes to strengthen your self-awareness, broaden your prospects, and motivate others with your positive influence.

HOW SUCCESSFUL PEOPLE WIN

Turn Every Setback into a Step Forward

No one wins at everything. But with this book John Maxwell will help you identify the invaluable life lessons that can be drawn from disappointing outcomes so you can turn every loss into a gain.

MAKE TODAY COUNT

The Secret of Your Success Is Determined by Your Daily Agenda

How can you know if you're making the most of today so you can have a better tomorrow? By following the twelve daily disciplines Maxwell describes in this book to give maximum impact in minimum time.

Available now from Center Street wherever books are sold.

Also available in Spanish and from hachette AUDIO and hachette DIGITAL

GET YOUR FREE MENTORING CALL
WITH
JOHN C. MAXWELL

Start setting goals to blow past your capacity today with a FREE mentoring call with John C. Maxwell. He'll equip you with the tools and practical thinking that will kick-start your journey to bigger goals, a better plan, and an intentional life.

MINUTE
WITH MAXWELL

Join me each and every day for "A Minute with Maxwell" as I inspire, challenge, and equip you with leadership teachings to apply to your life and career. I am excited to share my short, powerful, FREE video messages with YOU.

Words are vital to communication and leadership. "A Minute with Maxwell" will grow YOUR library of leadership words! Words like *teamwork*, *potential*, *strive*, *connection*, *clarity*—to name a few!

SO WHAT ARE YOU WAITING FOR?
www.JohnMaxwellTeam.com

Mobilizing Christian Leaders to Transform Their World

WHAT ARE WE GOING TO DO FOR PEOPLE WHO MAY NEVER COME TO CHURCH?

FIND OUT MORE HERE | www.iequip.church
678.225.3300

ACCELERATE YOUR BUSINESS RESULTS

People at all levels of an organization, not just the C-suite, have the ability to become effective leaders with proper training and commitment.

When you begin to invest in your human capital, watch what happens. Your workforce becomes aligned with your corporate initiatives. They begin supporting critical business priorities and change efforts, AND your business success begins to accelerate.

LEADERSHIP DEVELOPMENT

EMPLOYEE ENGAGEMENT

CHANGE MANAGEMENT

DOWNLOAD OUR FREE INFOGRAPHIC!

24 Proven Practices to Increase Employee Engagement
info.johnmaxwellcompany.com/increase-employee-engagement

The JOHN MAXWELL **Co.**
CORPORATE SOLUTIONS DIVISION

To learn more about our corporate training programs, contact our Corporate Solutions Division.
*Visit **johnmaxwellcompany.com** or call **678-387-2810**.*